Who'd You Put Your Panties on for Today?

by Amy Deans

ISBN: 978-0-6155932-9-6

Thank You

I have to thank myself first, for having the courage to share my story. It was not always an easy road, but well worth the journey.

Golden and Jordan, my two boys, who stood by me the whole way and gave me endless hugs and kisses, as well as unconditional encouragement.

My sweet husband, who supported my creative process as well as reminding me, when need be, to get back into my own panties and take time for myself.

Mom and Shauna, two of the very best friends I could ever ask for.

My sister and illustrator, Tara, who was able to put into a drawing what I was envisioning in my head and always did it so quickly.

All the gals of the women's council at work who listened to me talk panties the last 3 years and have cheered me on every step of the way.

Many, many others who have taken my hand during the moments in my life that I may have needed it most and reminded me gently of who I am when it may have slipped away from me.

And to those who I will share a smile with from this point forward.

Welcome to a New Way to Start Looking at YOUR Life

Contents

Introduction

For several years now, at least 20 or so, I have suffered from the disease of needing to please people. I had very minimal personal boundaries; I even changed myself for others with the idea I would be more "loveable", but became more angry and resentful every second of every minute of every day. In exchange for this behavior, my health suffered, I was irritable and those around me received the brunt of my continual overwhelm from always putting others needs, wants and desires before my own. Most onlookers would never have known I was fuming on the inside and searching for MYSELF in all I was giving away. I was the perfect "Blonde Barbie Doll"; beautiful on the outside but empty on the inside.

I knew this was not the way my life was supposed to be. I did not want to continue feeling such negative and harsh feelings for others. It wasn't their fault. After all, I was the one saying yes.

I started to dabble in Energy Psychology techniques such as NLP, Emotional Freedom Techniques, The Law of Attraction, body work, positive affirmations and healing myself. Even though I received new tools and additional benefits from each of these, there was still something missing for me. I wanted a way to prompt my consciousness, some kind of tangible reminder, to help me shift immediately when I was struggling with a negative thought or saying "yes" to doing for others when I really could not fit one more person, place or activity into my life.

My answer came in the form of two of my favorite things; a spin class and panties. I was spinning on a regular basis, building my muscles and giving my bottom a new lift. Bulking you could say, until I slimmed down. My mom made a casual comment that my butt and thighs looked bigger and thicker since starting my work out and, as a result, I did not return to my beloved spinning class for over a month.

Why did I allow someone's comment to affect me to the point of stopping something I loved and did for myself? This is when it occurred to me; everything about myself, down to the choice I made about what panties to put on each day, I did for someone else.

I was constantly wearing my panties for someone else.

With my new-found "panty awareness" I began to see how I eventually allowed myself to get stuck in a particular pair of worn-out panties. Unattractive, beat up, old and faded. There was a choker around my neck and a chain attached to it; strong, thick and long, allowing me to be pulled in every direction possible. My hands were free, so I could pull back once in awhile, but there was a ball in my mouth so I couldn't state my own opinion. I had chained myself to my beliefs from the past and wasn't even sure when the whole cycle had started.

This "panty awareness" gave me the perfect tool to help me remember my life was about me first. I came up with a question I asked myself every day, "Who am I putting my panties on for this morning?"

I am able to change a negative thought, a bad day, even a life experience by becoming more conscious of what I am putting next to my skin. If I am uncomfortable in a chosen pair of panties, if they have become wedged between my butt cheeks, I simply ask myself, "Why am I holding on to this particular pair and what is this uncomfortable experience representing in my life right now?" And am I willing to let that go?

There are hundreds of thousands of different styles, costs, colors, prints, materials and places to purchase panties. I use my older panties to rid myself of old beliefs. I take the specified pair and attach the old belief. At times, I even write my negative thoughts on the old panties with a sharpie and throw them in the trash. If the negative thought ever comes to haunt me again, I simply bring the visual back to my consciousness of disposing my panties with the old negative belief into the waste basket, thus quickly reminding myself there is no need to revisit those negative experiences again; I have disposed of them.

No matter what time of the day it is, if I am struggling with how I feel about myself or if I'm frustrated with something in my world, I simply adjust my mindset to my panties, noticing how they are physically touching my skin, how they are intimate and personal to me. Then I label them with a few simple, encouraging and inspiring words I may need for the day or sometimes even for a few hours.

I have realized if I am uncomfortable in a certain pair of panties, I am also uncomfortable in my own skin. I am able to change my attitude and my mindset within seconds with this fun, thought-provoking "panty awareness" daily. It keeps me pleasingly accountable for the many times I agree to something I just don't want to, blame others for my attitude or mood, and gently reminds me to ask for what I want.

This book is about breaking free, getting away from being so wrapped up in what others think of you, or the need to please others to the point you feel bound, chained and speechless.

You can't please everyone all of the time, so what are you doing wearing so many pairs of ill-fitting panties?

When I started asking myself, "Who'd you put your panties on for today?" my response was, Me, of course! I'm the one who opened my drawer and pulled out a pair and slipped them on. I bet the majority of us believe that until we really take a closer look at ourselves.

What I really encourage you to ask yourself is: Are you making a choice based on what you think others want from you or on what you want for yourself?

As women, we've all made choices based on what others want from us. No need to punish ourselves for our past...simply ask yourself, "Who'd you put your panties on for today?" Did you put your panties on for yourself, your dreams, and your decisions or did you put them on for those around you?

Remember it is your story!   ***Your panties!***   ***Your choice!***

(A Letter to Myself)

Hey Woman-

I had to write and tell you, I had yet another epiphany into the realm of self-discovery.

You know I have been spinning and loving it. Well, the other day when I saw mom at work, she made a comment about my butt and thighs; she did not like how they were looking since I have taken on this new method of working out. I don't know what it is about the words of a mother, but crazy thing, I actually stopped spinning for at least a month. It drives me crazy that at age 42 I am still making choices in my life based on what others say to me. I know I have come a long way, but obviously I am not quite there yet.

Well, today, I went back to spinning class and while I was dripping with sweat and lost in my own thoughts, a question came to my mind; "Who do I put my panties on for in the morning, how often and why?" It was so ironic because I wasn't wearing any panties; I had my padded biking shorts on. I wasn't blaming my mom. It just became so evident right then, how I frequently leave ME out of my life.

I know it seems so simple, but you know what? I realized this question alone is what I, you and millions of other women need to ask ourselves every time we change something or do something for someone else at the expense of our self. Oh my, I have done this for so long; I really look forward to making new choices and moving forward with a new awareness for taking care of my wants, needs and desires.

I have heard of this awesome century (100 mile) bike ride,'Little Red Riding Hood. It is an all female bike ride in Huntsville, Utah. Huntsville is on the way to Logan and absolutely serene and beautiful. I signed up for it and am going to do the entire100 miles. I can't wait! It is going to be such an accomplishment and reward to myself for starting to make choices just for me!

Amy Deans

Panty Overview

...Nowhere is it required YOU wear your panties for someone else. You are already valued!!!

Definition: *Clothes worn underneath: clothes worn beneath outer clothes, usually next to the skin, and not normally seen in public. (Webster's Dictionary)*

TAKE NOTE: *There is not a single word in the definition of panties, indicating our panties should be worn for someone other than ourselves!*

We can learn from this by starting to put them on for ourselves!

Brief History

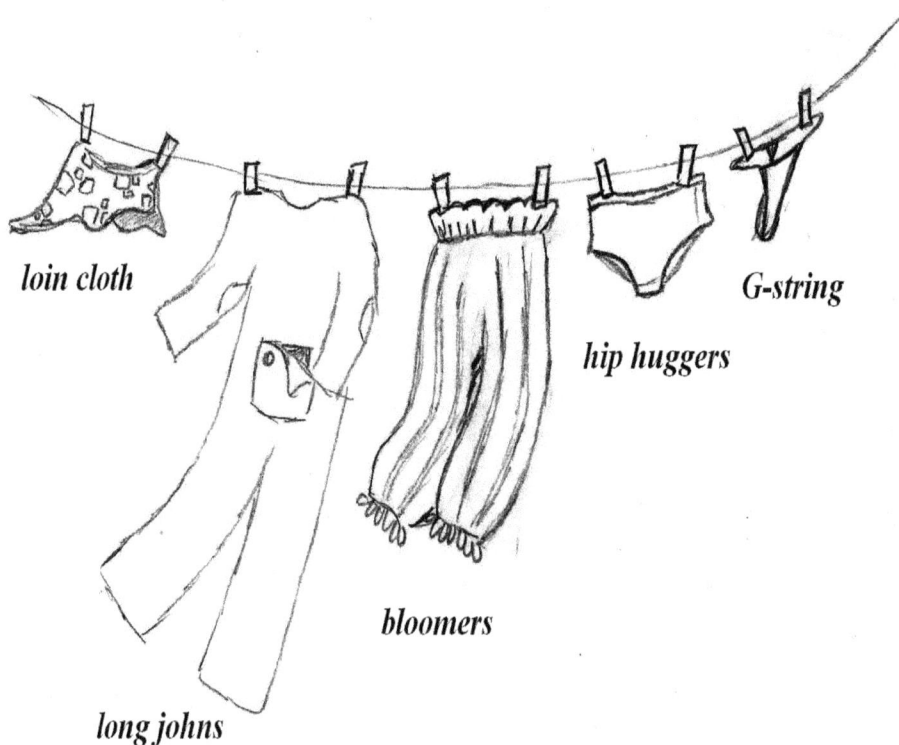

loin cloth

hip huggers

G-string

bloomers

long johns

Panty Styles

Classic Briefs

Hipsters

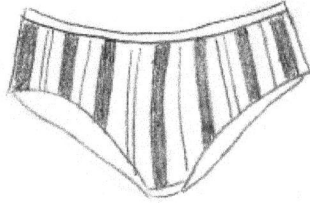

High Cut Briefs

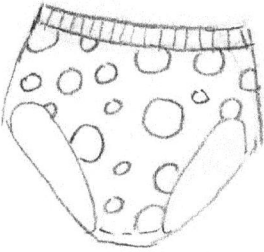

Bikini

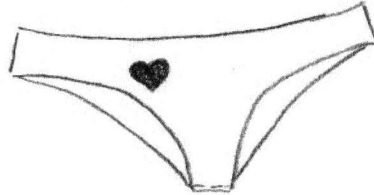

Thong

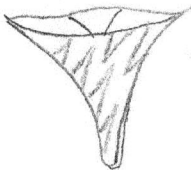

Boyshorts

Who'd You Put Your Panties on For Today?

Amy Deans

Panty Realization
&
Accountability

...it takes courage to grow and turn out to be who you really are...

Who'd You Put Your Panties on For Today?

My Journal Entries

I have the most exciting news; the boys are going to be moving in with Jeff and me full time. I have been waiting for this since Golden and I divorced 10 years ago. I have been working full time, but now I am working at home and it will be ideal because I can be a full time mom to them. It will be an adjustment for our marriage; with four children, we still have five days alone together.

It has been great to have the boys here with me. They are so much fun to have around and to I love being a mom to them both. I encourage them to make choices for themselves, especially when it comes to decisions like where they want to spend their money or what movie to go see. It is cute when I ask them, who do you wear your boxer shorts for? Their faces light up and they say, "oh yea, me". By the way, I want to write a book for men too, called, Who did you pull your boxers on for? There are men out there that give up a lot about themselves for someone else too. Oops, sorry I got off track there for a minute.

I have to say "YIKES" though to what is happening in my marriage. Jeff is really feeling left out in the scenario of me and the boys. When we talk about his feelings, I just get angry and frustrated; he just can't understand how important this is to me to have the kids around me now. I just want him to support me, being a mom. I feel like I am always thinking about him, his kids and their needs. It is hurting me and I feel very betrayed right now; my children are part of me even if they haven't been around for a majority of the time Jeff and I have been together.

I have been seeing a terrific counselor through EAP at work. She often brings things to my attention by asking me where I am accountable for the current conflict in our relationship. She asks me to focus on what Jeff is trying to do rather than on what isn't working for us. She reminds me I am dynamic and she says she enjoys seeing me because often times, I already have the answers to my own questions. I always leave her with a good feeling and am excited to go back and see her again so I can solve my own problems.

I am getting really tired and overwhelmed. I feel like I continue to walk down the same road and fall in the same hole over and over again. Jeff and I are at each other all of the time. If it is not about the kids, then it is about how little attention I am paying to him, the lack of sex or lack of trust, which by the way I created, as I continue to look outside our relationship for another to tell me how great I am. Jeff is just not accustomed to giving me compliments.

Jeff and I are now talking about separating. It just leaves me with such a sick feeling in my stomach, but things continue to get worse. I have been so spiteful, it scares me. We tried couples counseling, but Jeff does not seem as interested in it as me. He just does not do things like I do. I like the rugs straight and he likes them crooked. He likes late nights and beer and I want to be in bed by 10:00, so I can keep up with my life the next day. I am meticulous about the house being clean and he is great if it isn't. I don't want to do anything for him because I cannot see what he is doing for me. We are not communicating at all and I feel like I am talking to a wall because the garbage still isn't getting emptied when I want it to.

My tears frequently combine with the steam from a hot bath and soak the sheets at night when he is sleeping. I don't dare to express myself, as I am not sure it would make a difference right now. I'm not even sure I could state it in a way that I want him to understand or if it would end up in an argument because we now take the feedback we give each other as criticism.

I visualize myself in warn out, faded, tattered and torn leather bra and panty set. I have something stuck in my mouth and a collar around my neck. I have shackles on my feet only giving way enough for me to step forward and then I am pulled back again. I am not sure how I got here. I feel constricted, stuck.

8

We sat at lunch; I held an apartment finder magazine in my sweaty hands. I couldn't eat as we discussed where I should live and how to afford it. I had looked at a couple of places but they are icky, dirty, used, and expensive. We are cordial with each other and are almost sure this is the answer to all that currently ails us in our marriage, even though we cannot specify what it is that is splitting us apart.

I put some money down on an apartment about 10 blocks from our home. The complex is big, has a lot of lush green grass for the boys to play. The complex also has an indoor and outdoor pool for more entertainment and exercise. The manager informed me my application was accepted and the boys and I could move in on the 1st of the following month. She also encouraged me to start putting the utilities in my name.

I took Jordan to the apartment. It was on the third floor and in the corner of the complex. I walked him around the 800 square foot place we would be calling our new home and explained how we would set things up. Oh, it was so heart breaking; Jordan just started to cry and ran out the door and down to the car. He said he just can't live in an apartment! When we got home, I shared with Jeff what had just happened when Jordan and I were at the apartment. With my eyes welling up with tears, I asked if he thought we could work it out and if the kids and I could stay. I think it will be okay. I hope, I hope, I hope.

Jeff and I are okay. Nothing spectacular that is for sure. I still want him to be one way and he still wants me to stop straightening rugs and learn to relax more.

Combining families is tough. Not only is it the children but you have to throw the exes in the scenario, too. The kids are constantly comparing what they have to each other. They feel like nothing is fair. Goldie struggles with some anger and I am not sure how to handle it. Jeff gets so upset with the way the kids are treating me. I ask him to just let me handle it. We don't back each other up much. It feels like a tug-o war is happening all the time.

I feel like I only write about the bad things. However, bad seems to be the most prominent things in life right now. The great news about that is, I have lots of opportunities to remind myself to put my panties on for me.

I have sat down to write the last several days but every time I do, I get a deep ache in my chest. It almost feels like I am having a heart attack or as if a Clydesdale is standing on my chest. I have to be strong now, stronger than ever before, because this is now the third time Jeff and I have talked about me leaving. I can't wait around for him to ask me again. What does all of this mean; third strike and I am out? I can't even imagine how much more pain could happen if I continue to stay around.

There is such an interesting aspect to our relationships struggles, like it was all meant to happen right now. A man on the street below us recently passed away and one of Goldie's adult friends bought the home. The new owner has offered to rent it to me. He is planning to remodel and said that I can pick the colors and help in the re-designing of the home to my liking. This allows us to stay in Murray, in a home with a yard for the kids, same schools and friends. Jeff is fine with us staying until the home is ready. I am not sure when it will be finished, but Jeff and I have committed to spend Christmas together.

This is killing me on the inside; my heart is breaking every minute of every day. Jeff doesn't know. I have given up saying anything. When we were at Jordan's football game the other day, Jeff put his arms around my waist and asked me to stay. I just can't, I can't wait for the next time. I really thought the two of us would be together forever and support each other no matter what. No one would believe these things were happening between us. Not us, we are the perfect couple. Maybe pretending to be "perfect" was exactly the problem.

I have walked by the new house several times. I am not excited at all. I hold it all together so the kids believe I am making a choice that will work in the best interest of all of us. Most of the time my stomach gets queasy and the tears start to swell. I just wipe them aside before they touch my cheek and are visible to anyone. I walk forward and reassure the boys with a pat on the back and once again, remind them we are going to be great.

I sat in the driveway of our current home and talked for hours to mom about what I should or shouldn't do. I feel so torn, betrayed and disappointed. I knew this was an opportunity to put my panties on for myself, but they are not at all comfortable. Right now my panties are made of concrete. They are getting heavier and more protective. No one, no man, will ever get through to me again.

It sucks to be in this position. I know so much of my situation is because of my lack of self esteem and personal boundaries. Everything Jeff wanted, I simply did. Putting it into panty terms, I have been a chameleon changing to suit his every desire. I guess I figure that if I am all that he talks about, he will love me even more.

In October, I am starting work at the new hospital. It is actually within walking distance of the new place. It will be interesting to be working again, but I am excited. I will be the Medical Assistant in the Liver/Kidney/Pancreas Transplant clinic. My boss is outstanding, fun and very excited to have me there. I will still be doing all the medical transcription work at home. Oh boy, it will be so much to do on my own, but I can do it.

I didn't sleep well last night. More pain in my chest and the fearful thoughts continue invading my mind. The new house is painted and ready for us to move into. I feel like this is a bad time to be moving— December 15 to be exact. So close to Christmas. I think I am as ready as I will ever be. The song by Rascal Flatts "I Feel Bad that I

Don't Feel Bad?" runs over and over in my mind. I have definitely reached that point.

I made the move to the street below where I have been living for the last seven years, as a family, with Jeff and the kids. Jeff and Brian helped me and you know; it was really ok! We are both feeling good about this temporary separation knowing we are still married, but just in different households. The kids can grow up a little bit and we can learn to support each other better.

No one agrees with our decision because it does not fit the "traditional" description of marriage. You know what my answer is? I am no longer worried about what everyone else says, I am putting on my panties for myself. I explain it a little bit differently. I simply say, "Have you ever had a pair of underwear that just does not fit correctly? Day after day, you put them on expecting something to be different about the way they fit, but it is always the same?" Well, that is the point we have reached. Our relationship is uncomfortable and we are not willing to continue wearing the same uncomfortable pair of underwear anymore. We are going to try on something different and hopefully more flexible, which will allow us to breathe and feel more supported. There is no room for argument when I explain the situation in this way.

Being alone, without an adult man around, is going to be an interesting experience for me. I have always had a male someone there. In fact, I have always had more than one someone. I always had a back door open for escaping if my one someone didn't work.

It is important to me to always know I won't be left alone. I have a feeling this next little while, on my own, will be quite the learning experience. I certainly have created the space I need to put my panties on for me, and only me, every morning. Here I go!

I have made it a part of my morning ritual to ask myself who I am putting my panties on for today? I have started asking for what I want, doing more of what I want and saying "no" to what I would rather not do. It has been challenging because the people in my life

12

are used to the Amy who will take care of everything and make the situation work no matter what.

I have to say, life without a man is definitely a new experience for me and not nearly as bad as I imagined. I now have the opportunity to focus solely on me. I no longer have someone else to focus all my attention on. I really get to examine my own behavior and investigate why I have made, and continue to make, certain choices.

The other day when I got home from work, I walked in the house and immediately started in on the kids, asking them why their socks were on the floor and why the front room was not picked up. Goldie just looked at me and then said, "How about, it's good to see you and how was your day and thanks for what you did do". I just stood there! Wow! Talk about some powerful feedback and from a 14 year old none -the -less.

When Jordan and I were in the grocery store, he said to me, "Mom you have to have everything perfect in your life or you won't be happy." Yet another bit of powerful feedback for me to look at. I started to realize the high expectations I put on the people around me. If it is not the way that I do it, then it is not the right way. I have got to learn to relax and enjoy life more. If something is not in its proper place, it is not the end of the world.

I need to be careful not to be self abusing while I am being open to feedback. Some days are definitely easier than others. I came up with a great new way to inspire myself on the more challenging days. YES-it does have to do with my panties. Here is what I do. Let's say I wake up feeling upside down because I fell off the wrong side of the bed in the middle of the night. The thought of going to work is not so appealing. I worry that I might pop off and say some unkind words to another individual. When getting dressed, I pick my intimate under clothing with determination. Today, I chose a matching set. Black with a delicate lining of white lace around the edges, and I label them:

LOVING AND CARING!

It works so well. I think about them all day long because I can feel the material next to my skin. When I use the bathroom, which happens several times a day, I see the black material and it reminds me of my intention to be loving and caring. I grin and move forward with my day.

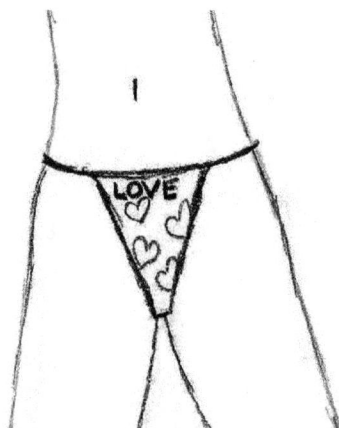

I do this on so many days or even for just a few moments. I can label my panties first thing in the morning or in the middle of the day if something comes up. I can re-label my panties with whatever affirmation I need at that time.

There are thousands of affirmative words out there. You can find them everywhere but I actually printed off a list of some I can use daily. I want to find a pair of panties specific to being spontaneous. After the feedback I have been receiving, I want to relax and let go. Maybe they could be made out of mesh for breathing room!

Work is always a fun experience. I hear stories from other women who have made similar choices and are constantly doing things for their spouse and their children, but they do not know how to ask for what they want! It is amazing to me. Oh my, you name it and I have heard it from someone around me.

How in the world do we get ourselves into these situations?

I realize I have been wearing an incredibly, non breathable, constricted pair of panties by keeping everything in my life so controlled. I am cleaning all the time, tracking finances and working all these different jobs at once. It is incredible I even remember what fun is and how to take time for me.

I have been taking classes at the community college but this time in my own panties. I am taking a Social Work class and a Family

14

and Marriage class. They are both informative and teaching me a lot about what has happened in our culture. I am realizing Jeff and I threw up our hands and let go of what we had in our relationship and then blamed other circumstances in our lives for our problems. No, it is US we need to be looking at. It has become so easy to get divorced that it seems people are taking the easy way out. I can even see, just by taking these classes, how I would project my insecurities on Jeff.

I was so particular about things, making it impossible for Jeff to ever meet the high expectations I had set for him. I wanted him to be like me. I had forgotten I fell in love with him because we had a lot of things in common and the things I thought I lacked (relaxation and spontaneity) he balanced in our relationship.

I have made choices for so long to protect myself from being alone, that I actually created being alone. Although it has been a great learning experience for me to experience life without a relationship and getting to know myself and why I make the choices I do. I feel like it is time to allow myself to be in a healthy, loving and giving relationship. It is time to break free of my strong, cement panties and put on a surrendering pair.

It is going on 10 months since Jeff and I have been living in separate houses; however, we continue to spend time together, talk on the phone and text. I decided to ask Jeff for one month where we don't talk at all.

I just want to be clear that I can make it on my own without a man. That I can put on my own self love panties, so I can share my love with Jeff and be willing to allow and accept the love he has for me. The month will be over on my birthday.

Sally, my counselor, told me about a couple of great books by Byron Katie. The first book I chose to read was <u>Loving What Is.</u> The book made me realize that while I focused all my attention on how I am constantly putting my panties on for others, I had overlooked the fact that I was also asking others to put their panties on for me by expecting things to be done—my way. Definitely not a win-win situation for anyone involved with me. "My panties or the highway" was the expectation for anyone involved with me; my spouse and even my children.

I started writing all the things I appreciate about myself, Jeff and our relationship. It feels good to be shifting my focus toward a healthy, appreciative and grateful look at life.

The month is over and I am more certain than ever that I am ready to be back home with Jeff. Loving him for who he is and loving myself for who I am. It makes all the difference knowing I have panties on that support me and realizing the only one that can truly do that, is me.

I am afraid I may have lost Jeff during this month without any contact. I think at times he may want me to just let go. In the past, I would have thought if that is what you want, then that is what I will do. I would just forget about what I want. Not this time, I am putting on some fighting panties and going for what I want. I want my family back together and the lifetime of love and happiness that I truly believe is available to Jeff and me.

Jeff is a little hesitant and I understand why he would be.

It has been a long year for both of us, taking a deep look inside ourselves and taking accountability for the parts of the relationship that did not work. What he took, what I took and what we both forgot to give to each other when times got rough. Next week we are going to start a six week marriage class. It is not the kind of class that focuses on the past panties but a class encouraging the couple to focus on our lives and love now. We will discover our love language; learn healthy communication techniques and how to get back to enjoying each other for the things we do share.

Today, I went and had energy work done-I feel like I have been wearing a pair of panties consisting of hundreds of chains hanging from the waist band and dragging on the ground. I know I have worked so hard to get where I am but there is obviously more work to be done.

After I finished, I felt so light and clear. I have finally figured out my reasons for keeping a back door open to head out when my life was rough and uncertain and why I did not feel that allowing only one man to love me was enough. I believed that if I made even one mistake, they would leave me. The chained panties kept me in a time warp. I was chained and stuck by my belief that the people in my life, who loved me, would also leave me and relationships are meant to be hard and challenging. Happiness was not a possibility. I figured it was something I learned by watching the relationships around me. My mom and my dad and the several divorces they have gone through.

No more chained panties dragging me down. Bright, free and airy is all I am feeling!

Life back at home has been fabulous. Jeff and I sat for hours and talked about all the things that had happened in the relationship. We were not defensive at all and now we have each other's back where the chillin's are concerned.

18

I throw him off every once in awhile because I am not hiding my feelings anymore. If I am angry, frustrated, sad, let down or need help, I let him know. Sometimes I will even phrase it and say, you know babe, right now I have my anger, flaming red hot, lace panties on and it is okay for me to feel angry! I will change into a soft, satin, pale yellow, loving pair after I feel what I am feeling. He seems to be able to take a step back when I approach it this way rather than taking it personally. He is understanding and allows me the space I need to feel what is happening. When I am ready to share with him, he is approachable with listening ears and an open, non defensive heart.

As the days go by, I create new panties for myself. One of my favorites is what I call the STROKE. I visualize a full body suit covered with soft fur and when I want to hear something nice about myself, I will ask for a stroke.

It makes asking for a compliment, if you can't seem to find one for yourself, enjoyable.

I also have the Wonder Woman pair I choose to switch into when I am scared to ask for something I want. I remind myself over and over; Wonder Woman did not fear anything, certainly not asking for something she wanted. So, I should go for it. Ask for what I want. No Fear, No Fear.

I make up my very own panties just for me and what I struggle with. This is what makes this so much fun. Anyone can take a simple pair of panties and turn them into what they want for the day.

I am on my way!!!

Every day it becomes easier and easier to wiz through different thoughts I might be having, re label my panties accordingly in seconds and make sure the person I am wearing them for is me. I notice the days I am living in the present and enjoying life, are the days I am not thinking of my panties at all.

The Panty Revolution blog is up and running. I have come up with all kinds of panty experiences. It has been so much fun to share them and post my thoughts. At the same time, I have had to come up with a new pair of panties to remind me if I am not writing, blogging, working, typing, being a mom and a wife, it is perfectly ok, I am still a worthy woman.

My life has become a different scenario than what I had lived in for three quarters of it. I ask for what I want and accept the assistance I am given, accepting it for what it is and what others have to offer in their own set of panties.

My ingenious and panty inspired revolution has begun.

Whose Panties are YOU Wearing?

...Intriguing how we remain concerned about what everyone else might think and forget about what we think of ourselves...

Who'd You Put Your Panties on For Today?

SO, WHOSE PANTIES ARE YOU WEARING?

Is it for the approval of your family?

Your Dad?

Your Mom?

Brother or sister?

What about your children?

The acceptance of a friend?

Boy/spouse/significant other?

Work/boss/co-workers?

Anyone and everyone? (is where I used to fit in)

All the little stuff?

Family

I find it easy to become consumed by the input and opinion of what my family may think of a choice I have made. They are of course, the individuals I have spent years with, as well as those I go to when I am struggling. However, as I have gracefully moved forward in life, I realize I am the one living with the choices I make and not them. Therefore, putting on my panties for me is essential.

Parents

I am intrigued, even though we are middle aged, we still find it necessary to please our parents and worry about what they think or how they might judge us for a decision we have made.

The voice of a parent forever sticks with you. Years later, you still remember their comments, even if you don't remember what you did to warrant the "feedback."

You're a grown up now. There is no longer a need to seek their approval. I KNOW they raised you and you appreciate them for the time and effort it took to do so, but cut the cord already. It is time to live your life for yourself.

Bloomers come to mind, the kind mom bought you. They typically are white, not much thrill to them. There is no doubt that this pair covers everything; full butt cheeks up to the belly button, catching air and inflating like a balloon in the space between your belly and the cotton material. Definitely not tight or sexy in the least way, like the special pair you spent your own allowance on and hid in the depths of your drawer.

Even though I know I could fill volumes with my own stories, it is important to me that I share the panty insights of other women as well. As you enjoy their insights, can you see yourself in their stories? What are your panty insights?

Panty Insights Regarding Mom

Recently my mother and I were shopping for dresses for my sister's wedding. As I was changing, my mom grabbed the extra skin around my belly and stated, "Looks like it's time to start working out." "Great, thank you for sharing," I thought to myself. Her words stick in my mind even to today as I strive for an hour glass figure that does not have any extras on the side. During that time, I felt like I had see-thru panties on, tight and gripping.

I would have rather been wearing baby blue, seamless, high cut cotton briefs.

T.A., Arizona

I was texting my good friend telling her that my boyfriend and I were going on a little vacation together and mentioned to her, "Yes, we are staying in the same room, but don't tell my mom." She texted back — "I'm calling her right now." It took me back for a moment and I really questioned why it was that in times like this, I slip back into my big, tattered and torn bloomers that she used to buy me when I was growing up, to please her. I'm 40 years old!

I would have rather been wearing my silky, leopard print, barely there string bikini panties.

G.R., Idaho

After the earthquake in Haiti, it came to me that I would like to adopt a child from there and make her part of my family here in Salt Lake. I am a single mom with three older children. The one thing that makes me so nervous is telling my mom. Not only is she my mom but she is also my best friend and I value her feedback. I am really scared to tell her. My "fear" panties are strangling my thought process and my optimism.

Today is a day that I have created a steel pair of panties to keep criticisms out and be happy about my own decisions to move forward with the adoption.

C.M., Utah

You wouldn't think that being married, with five children and having your oldest daughter getting married, I would still be subject to the old feelings of guilt when my own Mother commented on my wedding attire.

I had chosen a silk blouse and skirt and jacket, it was a garden wedding. It was mid July and above 90 degrees, a bit hot, so the jacket spent most of the afternoon on a chair.

Much to the embarrassment of my Mother, I had chosen in my mind a very feminine lacy bra to wear under my blouse. (mmmmm a bit too revealing I guess for my ultra modest "Mom")

To this day almost 25 years later I frequently recall the flush on my cheeks, when she raised her eyebrow and commented "you can see thru your blouse". Nothing more was said, however I made a quick visit to the mirror in the nearest restroom to check and see if I was looking a bit too "revealed", then for my Mother's sake, I donned my jacket.

I still love the silk blouse and now I can wear the lacy bra without a qualm with or without the jacket, it's me at my most feminine!

D.O., Utah

As long as I am visiting the parents today I may as well stop by Moms place and see what's up. Then it dawns on me like it always does. That pair of oh so tattered and sentimental panties that call to me, are the ones that always crawl right up my butt crack until I go stark raving mad. I always forget until it's too late, but I just can't seem to part with the old girls.

Today, I have on white lace high cut briefs.

W.G., Utah

The first pair of panties I can remember were ruffled white panties I wore with my church dress. They had to be pretty panties, in case I bent over and anyone who was at church with us could see that I was well groomed and dressed. I also had white ruffle socks and white gloves, As I progressed through my pre-school years, I was given a purse and hat that would add to my outfit at Easter.

As I went through my elementary years, I had nice panties to wear to school under my school dresses, since when I went to school, girls were not allowed to wear pants. When I would get home off came my public outfit down to my panties, and I would put on my play clothes. The after school outfit included pants, so I would even change from my good panties, to the old ones that weren't nice enough to be worn under a dress.

As a young married adult I wore panties under a girdle. There I was tall 5'10" and only 125lbs., but I felt the need to reign myself in, in every way imaginable. My husband was a very controlling man, and I was young and weak enough to let him. I lived that way for several years wearing whatever panties I thought was wanted by others, synthetic, scratchy lace, panties that would ride up, just so they looked good.

Finally, I got to the point in my life that I decided to be myself. White cotton Haynes for Her. They fit well, don't ride up and the cotton lets you breath. So until this last chapter in my life, my panties reflected the needs of those around me. Now those close to me fit me well, they don't constrict and they let me breath.

Life is truly like the panties you wear!

D.L., Utah

Panty Insights Regarding Dad

I was heading to my dad's house. Dang, I forgot to put on my regulation tighty-whities. Oh yea, that's right, I don't own any. I guess he will just have to deal with whatever happens to be clean in the basket today. Besides, he can spot a happy go lucky fly by the seat of her pants daughter anyway no matter what I wear. I'm afraid it's a burden he shall have to carry and learn to deal with, sorry Pops!

W.G., Utah

I pretty much wore panties made out of egg shells whenever I think about my relationship with my dad. He was used to having everything just perfect. I remember that if I even let the water get on the sidewalk when I was watering the lawn then all you know what would break loose.

I knew that I could not live in crusty shells forever, so I broke out of them and moved into a pair of relax fit, freely moving bright pink cotton briefs.

J.F., Texas

For a lot of years, I felt like I wore armor for my panties. I hid my feelings and love for others, just like what I saw from my own father. Not very often did I hear him tell me that he loved me. When I did I treasured those time, but I know that it still made me guarded from having and expressing my own feelings.

I took the metal cutters to those babies, and got myself into some panties that stated little expressions on them, just so I could start allowing myself those feelings. Today, I am able to express numerous feelings! And I love it.

L.F., Washington

It is funny, before I was asked this question, I had never really thought about it. I realized that when I am home and wanting to spend time with my dad, I just do what he wants to do. He is not very active so I find myself just sitting there watching T.V. with him, just hanging out in a pair of old long johns.

After I wrote this, I headed for a little spandex and invited him to do some physical activity, even if it is a little bit of bowling on the WII.

T.D., Utah

Panty Insights from the Family

I am worried about what my brother is going to say. I always laugh when I am at his house because he has a picture on his fridge of Tom. I used to say that if Tom and I ever split up that he would disown me and keep Tom in the family—we will see what happens now. It is an opportunity for me to remember, who I put my panties on for in the morning.

I have to get out of my brothers XL boxer shorts and put on my own silky, canary yellow, true fit seamless hipsters.

A.R., Minnesota

Every year I head back home to spend a glorious vacation with my family. In the months before our annual meeting, I start wearing my panties for them and worry about what they think of me. They are "thin", whatever that means, and I am not, according to their standards. All the sudden, I head into major dieting and exercising to try to meet their expectations, and every year, I try to fit into their panties...

From this year forward, it is into my own marine green, lace trimmed nylon briefs I will be packing in my suitcase.

J.F., Montana

I have been through many break ups and even move outs with my current husband. My family has always listened to me and been there for me, when I have been hurting, and I know that they do not support me reuniting with him any time in the future after the pain they have watched me go through. I have been torn for a long time. I really want my family to be together; me my husband and our children. However, I have been trapped in a pair of "what will they think of me" panties if I reunite with my husband. ·

I was able to get clear about what was really important to me and my life. Even though I am grateful for the input they have always given me, I put on "it is my choice" panties and I chose to get back with my husband and we are happy as can be now.

M.C., Oregano

I had been struggling with some financial issues when my parents told me they wanted me and the kids to join them on a family vacation to Europe. I felt so much pressure to go with them and I knew that the kids would really enjoy the time with them as well, and what an opportunity to visit a place out of the Country. They continued to talk to me about it and pressure me. I felt like I was wearing two pair of underwear, and neither one of them were from my drawer. I continued to express my financial concerns, and they continued to ask that I go.

It took a little bit, but I was finally able to shed myself of their desires and put on my own, "I'm going to stay at home", forest green, soft cotton bikini briefs.

V.S., Washington

Christmas has always been a big celebration time for the family. Not just my family but the WHOLE family, and I usually am more than happy to host it. This year, once again, the family asked me to get in my red velvet, tinseled boyshorts, elf hat and host the party. I really do enjoy doing this but this year, I have too many other things going on and the thought of putting everything together is overwhelming me and I am noticing that I am agitated because I have not been able to tell them "No" yet.

I put on my "I am going to take care of myself", basic white spandex high cut briefs and made the phone call to my mom to let her know that I would not be the one to host this year. She was understanding and encouraged me to take care of me and that all would be well and taken care of if I was not the one that did it all.

A.D., Utah

I have been dating my boyfriend now for over 6 years, recently we decided to combine income and our stuff and move in together. Even though my family is cordial to my boyfriend, they do not think he is the "right" one for me and clearly state this too me on every outing that I visit with them. When Jordan and I made this decision, I was stuck in my "I don't dare to tell them" panties. Constricting little buggers that is for sure!

It took me until after the move in that I was able to slide into a pair of "I am old enough to make my own decisions" orange and yellow mesh thong. Even though they did not necessarily agree with the decision, they respected me for telling them.

I.F., Idaho

Who'd You Put Your Panties on For Today?

Children

Question: How do you keep your children from consuming your thoughts when they have made a choice you would not have?

Answer: Get out of their undies.

Panty Insights Regarding Our Children

I had not seen my daughter for a couple of years now, so we set up a dinner date to meet, spend some time together and chat about what has happened during that lapsed time. Wouldn't you know it, she stood me up. I felt like I had on a pair of bright red g-string panties blaring out my fury that she didn't even bother to call and let me know that she wasn't coming....I know that I taught her better than that.

I would have rather been wearing a basic beige tailored nylon briefs.

R.H., Hawaii

I got a clear picture of what it feels like to be wearing a pair of size medium, snowboarding 11-year-old-boy's Haines boxer briefs this last week. I had to rush Jordan up to Primary Children's hospital as his appendix decided to burst. He was actually in the hospital for almost five days. I think he loved the attention and the fact that the nurses did for him whatever he wanted and he didn't even have to say please or thank you. Well, the little prince continued to demand things when we got home, until I reminded him that he is no longer at the hospital and that I would now be giving him back his boxer shorts!

I was now in my own pair of gray and pink polka dotted, oh so comfy, no demand spandex boy-shorts.

Please and thank you are the words you use to get things in our house. He just smiled. He knew what he was doing.

A.D., Utah

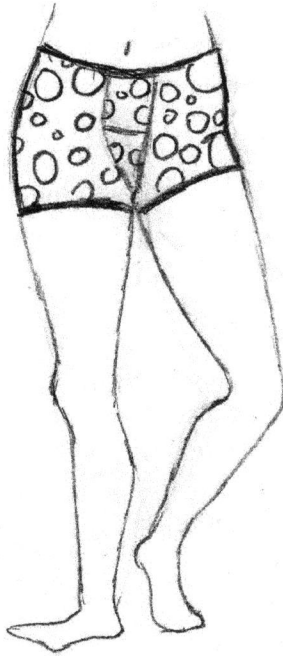

Ah, 12 years old and going on 13. I get "Ugggg" more than I get, "You betchya, Mom." when asked to do anything other than sit there and do nothing, hang with friends, or play sports, eat or listen to music. I have just got to get these tighty-whitey briefs off!!!

It is a good thing that I have a pair of flowered, mint green and brown laced patience bikini panties.

A.D., Utah

There is always a little of pain when I tell my children that tonight is a night just for me to spend with my husband for a little bit of alone time. I can hear it in their voice that they are disappointed. However, when you run around with just a piece of each of their undies on, I have to get out for a little alone time with my hubby.

Tonight is a night for all lace, magenta, no-worry hipsters.

J.R., California

I am one of those lucky moms that seems to always have one of my children living with me even well after the time that the general society thinks that they should. This time it's my daughter, her husband and my brand new grand baby. I absolutely love them all. However, as they lived in my home they forgot to take care of some of the basic needs of the home....like cleaning up after themselves. I felt like every time I wanted to even get my panties in to wash them, there was still left over clothes filling the washer bin and smelling like they had been there over night, you know that smell?

It took me a minute to state what my needs were. I felt conflicted and wanted them to know that they were welcome there but at the same time, I had expectations of them and knew that I wanted to let them know what those were. If they chose to leave because I have boundaries, then so be it.

I knew I could make it a win win situation, but I would have to get into my win panties and express to them my wants also.

T.K., North Dakota

Combining two families has really been one of the most difficult things that I have ever done. Not only have I been parenting my two children, but just this last year, my husband's two children also moved in and I now do the majority of the parenting with them also, as my husband works most of the time and is not available to do this. Even though I absolutely love having all the family in one place, at times it is very stressful to always keep everything on the up and up. I find myself, more often than not, stuck in four different pair of panties and a pair of men's boxer shorts.

I'd rather be wearing my "remember your patience" panties that are flexible, army green and ever so comfy!

H.M., Montana

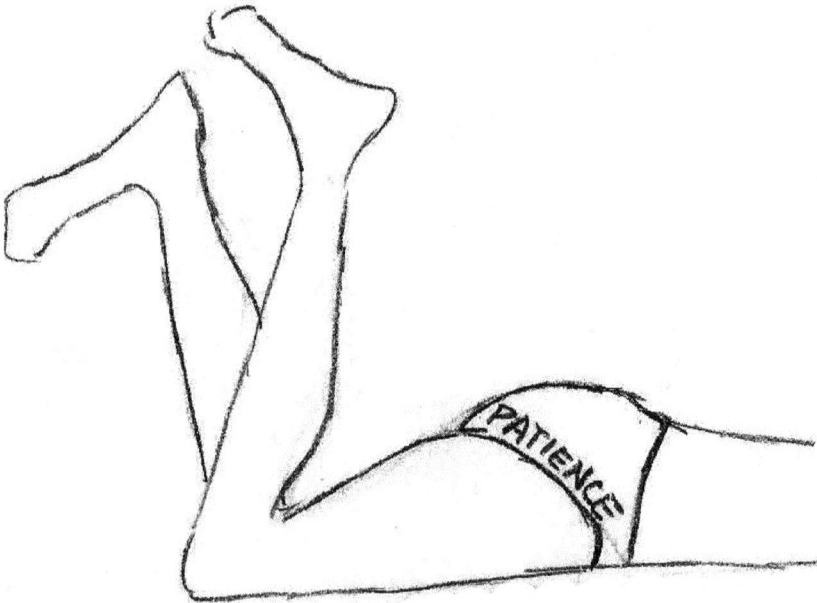

Peers/Friends

Friends are one of the greatest gifts we have been given. I think it is easy to get lost in what our friends want rather than what we want. I am not talking about the times we hangout to simply enjoy each other's company, I'm talking about when we have not created a space to say, I just can't do that today (without feeling guilt or pressure.)

Panty Insights Regarding Friends

Last night we hung out with a group of our friends As we laughed and enjoyed the evening, I started to feel sleepy. Thoughts of what I needed to accomplish the next day filled my mind and I wanted to get to bed. I sat there for another 20 minutes or so, feeling uptight and a little self-conscious about being the first one to leave the party. Basically I was sitting in all their undies, and not my own and let me tell you, it became very uncomfortable. I knew that it was time to get out of their panties and get on my own "ready for bed" panties. If not, I would become so irritated that I pushed myself to the limit.

I said good night and headed to bed in my cotton bikini briefs and tank top.

T.S. Nevada

Since high school, Jodi and I have been best friends. That is a lot of time for two people to confide in each other and have different experiences together, good and bad, (many of those when we were in high school.) We had a pattern in our relationship. I was the one that arranged things and waited for her to make up her mind about what she wanted to do. I would wait and wait and wait, putting my life on hold until she would make up her mind. At first, that was okay, but after a while, I felt resentful and I decided that waiting for what she decided to do, no longer worked for me. I felt a very strange obligation for years though, one that continued to keep me stuck and angry. I guess I felt like I owed her something for always being there for me.

It took me a long time to break out of the panties keeping us together and let her know that my time was valuable. I set a boundary and told her that if we were to do things together, that I would need a committed answer from her a couple of days ahead of time.

R.G., Wyoming

I have one friend that enjoys the night life and partying substantially more than I do. For awhile there, I did my best to keep up with her and enjoy the same things that she did. I finally realized however, that I did not enjoy being in her silver, glittery go-go panties and that is okay with me.

I graciously handed them back to her and let her know that I would be throwing my glittery panties away and coming a little more down to earth in a pair of silky, lavender thongs.

D.K., Maine

Work, Boss, Co-workers

Most of us head out of our home each morning to face a day at WORK. We have the opportunity to interact and communicate with many different individuals for at least 8 hours a day, 5 days a week. I have yet to experience a full week without the opportunity to look at my panties in relationship to the feedback I obtain from others while on the job.

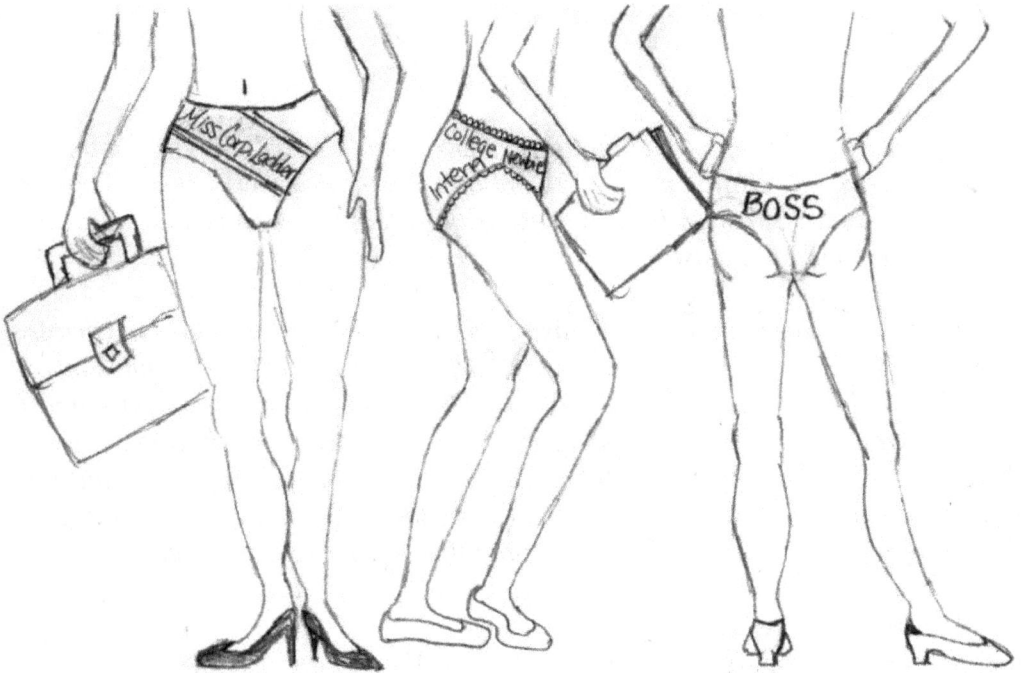

Panty Insights about Working

I enjoy my job, but there always seems to be one individual that stirs things up making it miserable for everyone else. My panties get all tangled up with this. "People are talking about me, AGGGGG. Why here? And why now? And why are my panties in such a huge twist over a pot stirrer?" So, in my mind I visually slide out of my panties, shake them out, straightened them and then put them back on, hike up the stairs and move on with my day.

T.D., Wyoming

My favorite, very prestigious Hepatology/Liver Transplant physician has made the choice to leave our clinic and head to another hospital across town and guess what, he asked me to go with him. I was so honored; he was asking me of all people to be his Medical Assistant at his new clinic.

Oh my! I knew immediately what my answer was. I didn't want to go for various reasons. His new clinic was across town and my kids are just three minutes away from the hospital I work at. I am not interested in working at a big hospital and I knew in my heart that I would not be doing this kind of work much longer. Even with all this in the back of my mind, knowing with my entire being that I did not want to work at a different hospital, I still wrote down the contact information of the gal doing the hiring and set up an appointment to meet with her. I did not know how to tell my physician NO, (but thank you!)

So, I spent the next few days asking others what they thought I should do. I did not hear any answers that coincided with the one that I already knew. Instead, I listened to everyone tell me I should at least check it out and see what the options are. Come on people, I just need one person to confirm what I have already decided. I finally brought it up with Sally. She just looked at me and asked, "Who did you put your panties on for Amy?" Nice point!

Because I was so flattered and honored by the offer of Dr. Box, I forgot to think about me. Once I was reminded of who I should be making my choices for, it was easier to tell him how much I appreciated the offer, but would have to pass.

A.D., Utah

The hardest part of my job is interacting with my boss. I know that there are certain rules that need to be followed and he has a hard enough job to do, but sometimes I find myself in the tightest most uncomfortable pair of panties ever because I feel like I cannot openly express my feelings about my position, thus causing conflict between the two of us. I squirm and squirm in my work chair and at times will even make a sarcastic comment about the way he does things around the work area. It is uncomfortable....

From now on, I want to get into a pair of specially tailored panties that remind me that he has a job to do and not to take things personally.

G.R., Texas

I have worked for the same organization for the last 24 years. Lately, there has been a lot of tension there because of the way things have been handled with the higher ups. There have been more times than not that I just dread coming to work because of the tension that fills the halls there. Even though I have years and years behind me with this particular job, I feel like I am trapped in a jail....I

am noticing that there is nothing that is rewarding to me there any longer. The hours are long, the patrons are unappreciative and my boss is inconsistent.

It is time for me to get out of the striped jail panties. I have found a new job, with flexible hours and people that appreciate my ability to take excellent care of them.

C.D., California

Boys/Spouse/ Significant other

Boy, oh Boy, Oh Boys how I want you to like me. What can I change about me for you?

This is one of the easiest places to find yourself making changes just for him. It may not always happen on a conscious level and it may take a minute before you realize you have done this, but know this from a professional; YOU can reclaim the panties you so graciously gave him and put them back on YOU!

Panty Insights Regarding Boys

When my spouse and I started being intimate with each other, while we were dating, his biggest complaint was my ugly cotton panties. Right then and there a major and uncomfortable change was made in my panty drawer. Most everything to do with our lives is like that panty drawer; If it makes him uncomfortable or makes him complain, then I can change whatever I can, no matter how uncomfortable for myself it may be. After his father died, the smallest pair of red satin thongs were brought out of the drawer and worn on a daily basis. That pair was the peace maker.

I have recently gone back to the comfort of cotton because I want to. Life is made for living and I'm going to do it in my cotton panties for me.

T.S., Utah

I visualize the panties that I've put on to please men sexually, to be as skimpy as possible, very uncomfortable and not my style at all. I am all about comfort. I don't like a thong up my butt, nor do I like having to objectify myself for "love."

Sex is NOT love. I want more from a man than good sex. I am MORE than a life support system for a vagina. Thong underwear is definitely not me.

I am a pair of cotton boy cuts...white, with pink trim.

S.V., Colorado

Ok well.... I gave up a lot for a guy but just one guy, family, country, friends and some of myself (beliefs, ambitions, self-esteem especially in regards to sex to please him). To me, at the time, I wasn't giving things up, but changing direction, until he started to take advantage and wasn't giving the same in return.

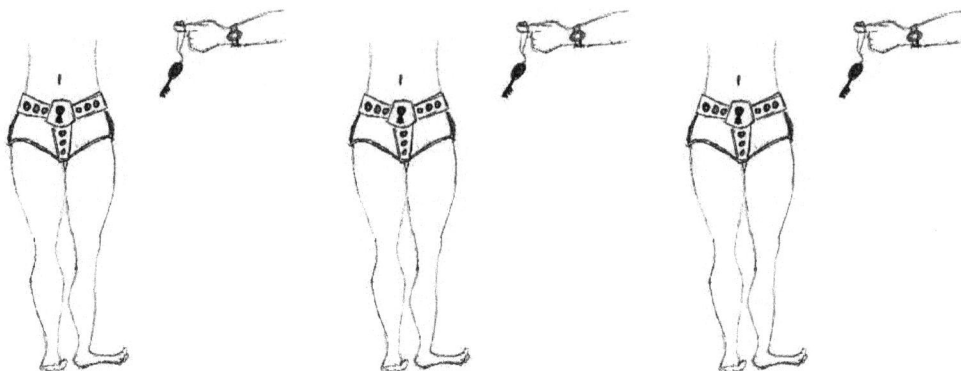

It became a very controlling relationship where he could have his cake and eat too. But not me, so I would say it felt like I was wearing a chastity belt (big, metal and heavy), one that only he had the key to. Trapped in the chastity belt I let him put on me

I would have preferred to be wearing something that made me feel sexy maybe black lace boyshorts or I like the classic thong (as long as it fits right)...

N.S., Utah

Mmmm.......well I think the one time I really gave up something about myself for someone else is when Jake went on his mission. I felt like since he couldn't go out & do things, that I couldn't go out & do the things that he couldn't do. I felt guilty anytime I had fun or did something that he couldn't do on his mission. I would say that at that time I was wearing a giant pair of granny panties. In fact, they were so big that I wrapped them around my entire body & hid inside of them for two whole years. Think of a turtle hiding inside of its shell with just its eyes peaking out. This was me looking out of my granny panties.

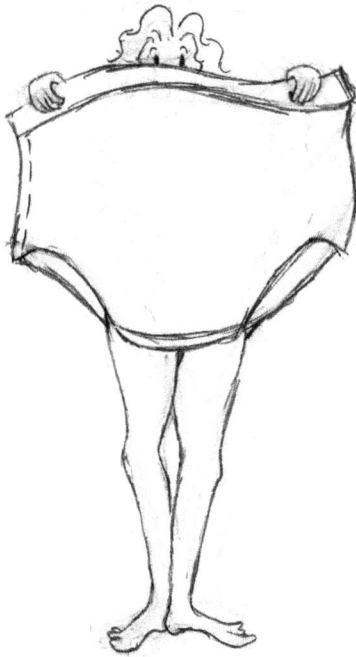

If I could go back & change I would go for not wearing any underwear. I was only 19 at the time & I should have been free to have fun, be wild, meet new people & propel my life forward. Picture me on top of a mountain in my naked glory facing the world with confidence, ready to take it on.

B.G., Utah

The best story I can think of was when I was leaving a serious relationship. My guy had cheated on me. Somehow, this betrayal forced me to step out of the strange fog I'd lived in my whole life and I began to grow into the person I truly am. It's a sad-ish story with the best ending. It was a long and painful journey but every step facilitated my growth and evolution and I wouldn't have it any other way. My ex, the cheater, liked a very uncomfortable skimpy thong. Apparently he needed a lot of panties from several women to be satisfied.

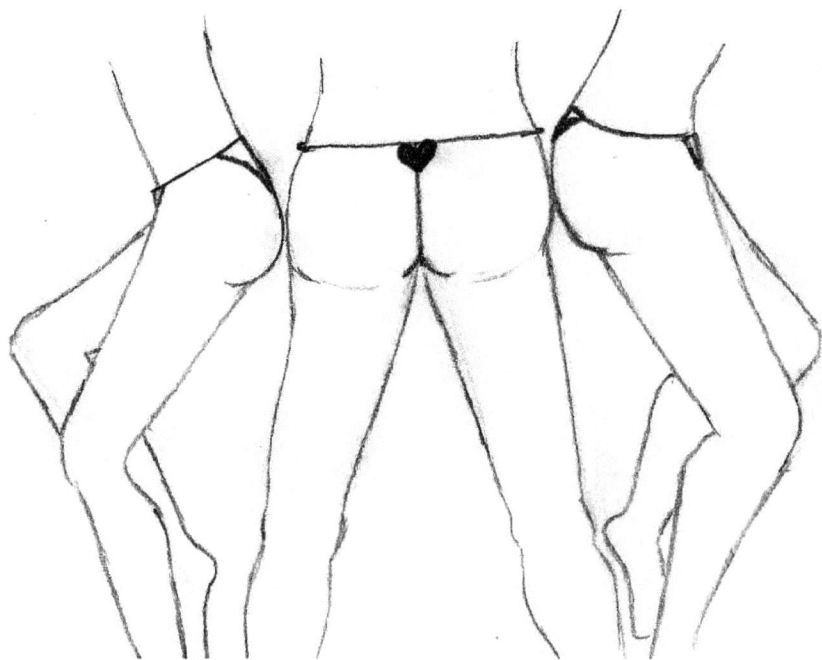

I know who I am today. I am a strong, hardworking woman who I love. I am on a path that continues to rise and evolve and am grateful everyday for learning what I have. My bright, crazy print and sometimes funky panties go on for me these days... Although I do have some naughty ones for my husband now. I guess they're part of a healthy me, too, as he does not require any of that from me.

G.S., Utah

Anyone/Everyone

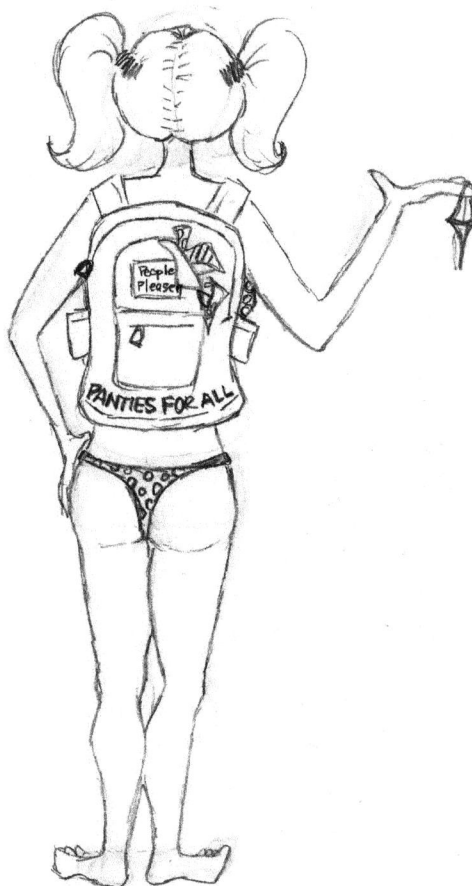

I just returned from a river trip with the gals. I am one of 25 women who venture to Moab for a crazy wild ride down the Colorado River. I have gone for the past 3 years and realize today why I am so incredibly fond of the time away. The guides, while we are on the river, take care of us, and I don't have to do a single thing I don't want to. No dishes, no children, no work, school, hubby or dogs to take care of. No dinners to plan or cleaning up to do. I can just BE and not worry.

Wow, how I get clear laying there next to river and staring up into a clear sky filled with stars, I just really want someone to take care of me the way I take care of the rest of the world. It feels awesome and actually, now I think about it, I just want to be able to take care of myself and put as much effort into my own care as I do everyone around me.

Panty Insights Regarding Anyone/Everyone

This happens to me every single time I throw a party. We always have an annual Halloween party and every year we go through the same thing; choosing a date so everyone can attend, when we don't have the kids, when hunting starts, the beginning of the month or closer to Halloween?

It is seriously a pain and to top that, when I finally have all the invitations out, stress over cleaning the house, decorating it, buying an excessive amount of beverages, and plates with matching napkins that say "BOO" on them, 5 people out of the 30 who promised they would come, show up.

NO more multicolored, ragged panties for me. I will find me a pair of black and orange spandex tailored hipsters.

A.D., Utah

I've got the panties of many colors thing going when I think of my relationships out and about, Look out Donny Osmond! My Panties, like my moods and dreams change as I do, every day with who it is I am hanging out with for the day. If they like clam chowder that day, so do I and if they want to see a movie that is a drama, then so do I. I do not always notice that I do this.

I would love to get into one solid color, navy blue, string bikini pair of panties so I can start making my own choices.

W.G., Utah

A couple weeks ago I went to an outdoor concert with my husband and a big group of friends. I decided to wear a summery, thin, grey dress and thus felt that I needed to put on some control top panties to hold everything in and feel confident. This concert was a pretty big deal and we met up with everyone early in the day for the pre party before the show. As we were standing in line to get dinner one of our girlfriends said, "hey, I really like your black thong".

I was astounded. Was my dress see through? Had the rest of the thousands of concertgoers also enjoyed the view of my black thong? Is that the reason I had been receiving comments, looks and touches? I was mortified and embarrassed and even more so because I was wearing the control top panties. If people were going to be seeing my underwear, I at least wanted to be wearing something from usual variety—a sexy low rise g-string or lace lined cheeked —-not some big granny looking control top black thong up to my belly button.

I guess the lesson learned is that you can't always be in control by wearing control top panties. The panties that I wore to try to control and manage my body, actually turned out to do the opposite---embarrass and misrepresent me.

J.B., Utah

Who'd You Put Your Panties on For Today?

Even the little stuff

My girlfriend and I were out walking on our lunch break and started discussing how it is that most women tend to conform into what we "think" or what we have heard our significant other express that he likes! We realized in the beginning of the relationship it is because we want them to like us, so we change even the littlest things about ourselves without thinking much about what we are doing.

I shared a story with her about the day I looked at my self in the mirror and reflecting back at me was a brunette with freckles! "Why the hell have I changed to being a brunette, when my whole life I have been a blonde?"(….ah yes, I remember, he once stated he likes brunettes and has never dated a blonde)

She told me how a thought struck her when she was on the freeway today with "Nine Inch Nails" squealing from the stereo speakers and rattling her brains to the point she couldn't even focus on what was in front of her. It dawned on her; she couldn't remember the last time she listened to the type of music she really enjoyed, down home Australian, Keith Urban.

We both giggled, as we became more aware and confided more little things to each other that we thought about or did change, all the way to the color of toenail polish we applied.

We have all done this at one time or another; changed something little for someone else.

What makes this unique for you, you ask?

You are aware of the choice you are making.

Make your next, and all new choices, the one that works for you.

Panty Insights about the Little Stuff

My 6 year old piano student told me I have monkey ears. I politely told her that they are elf ears and I think they are cute. She was insistent that they were monkey ears and they were funny looking. I'm suddenly feeling the need for an ear tuck.

B.G., Utah

I had my feet up on a table and my nephew was laying below my legs. He reached up & wiggled my calf "muscle" back and forth. He made a face in disgust & said "Ewwwww! It's like liquid." I promptly did 200 calf raises & committed myself to a life of running to firm up those liquid calves of mine.

B.G., Utah

For my sister's wedding, I had to curl my eyelashes on her wedding day or she would take away my "Maid of Honor" title. Of course I obliged. Otherwise, I wouldn't have a reason to wear that beautiful dress!

R.J., Nevada

Yesterday as I was reaching for something up in the cupboard. My husband smiled at me and said, hey, looks like you might be heading toward the lunch room soon. What he meant, was they ere sagging! I immediately headed to the weight room and started some tricep push backs. I'll show him, I thought.

A.D., Utah

Each quarter when I am deciding what classes that I want to take in college, I start to evaluate everyone else's schedule but my own, which leads me into choosing classes that I really would rather not take. Therefore, this term, I will pick the classes I want to take and go for it!

M.A., Idaho

A couple of months ago I went in for a partial hysterectomy as my moods and hormones were all over the place. The doctor only removed one of my ovaries but I continued to have this feeling that he should have taken both. He just continued telling me that I was too young. So, I went through with the surgery and the removal of only one ovary. Well, now the other one needs to come out. I walked in his office today and told him that he would be the one to pay for the surgery, as I had told him before that I knew they both should have come out. It felt so good to let him know how I felt and stand up for myself.

S.V., Colorado

When I was dating my husband, we were engaged actually, and we were talking about my hair and what I should do for our wedding. He made mention that he thought it would be pretty all blonde. At the time my hair was mostly blonde, but had dark red/ brown colors on the bottom and highlights of that throughout. It had become a favorite color style for me after years of being my friends guinea pig during the beginning of her cosmetology career. I had tried several color and cut styles over the years and had settled on this blonde and red/brown combo for a while and loved it. Here I found myself in a moment of pure infatuation and being so wrapped up in love, and "I'd do anything for you" feelings... So what do I do??

I ask my friend to bleach out my hair so I can be blonde! It turned out really cute and I was happy with it...or so I thought. Looking back at my wedding pictures I think to myself "Why did I change my hair for him? I loved my blonde/red combo and that was ME." My wedding pictures were wonderful, I looked beautiful and I don't regret anything about that special day. I have just learned over 7 years that I will do what I want with my hair and he will just need to be ok with it. I know my husband loves me for me and I don't need to change my hair for him.

A.M., Utah

This is a little personal, but I have always heard that men really enjoy woman who have a Brazilian wax. I had never thought about doing that but since I always want to please my man, I tried it. It felt so weird to me that night after I had a visit with my waxing gal. He actually didn't even have that much to say about it. What was I thinking?

K.C., Arizona

When I was in high school, there was a big swimming pool party that I was invited to. I was so excited until I tried on my swim suit. The top part, where breasts were supposed to be, just hung there; I literally had a AAA cup size. I headed to the store for some Styrofoam inserts. I looked great and the top fit perfect. Until, I jumped in the pool. Out popped my inserts and to the top of the pool they floated. I think it would have been better to go with the AAA size than mortification.

J.D., California

For me, I feel like I am always worried about my image. If I am not sucking in my stomach, than I am buying the most expensive creams that claim to smooth out any strange dimples in my legs. I know it is because I am growing older and it seems like heads are always turning toward the younger gals. I challenge myself to not get so wrapped up in it, and I do succeed at times. The great news is that I know that I want to feel secure enough with myself to just be who I am.

D.A., North Dakota

When I was in college, I had had several dates with this one fella. We were sitting on a porch swing next to each other and I had on a white button down, cotton shirt. I guess he could see a stitch of my white bra because he made a comment about me always having a white bra on and asked me, if I only had white bras. When I left there, I stopped by Macy's and picked me up a black bra.

V.Y., Utah

I have definitely changed my plans for others. I have had times when I had my whole evening planned and then I received a call from a special person that I just wanted to spend time with, so out with the previous commitment, in with a drive down town.

R.V., Nevada

My husband and I met at our place of employment. He had been working there for about 16 years and I was just in my first couple, and really enjoying it. After he found another job, he continued to talk about wanting to get me out of there. I finally gave in and left, even though I really liked what I was doing.

T.S., Florida

I was on my way to take a final test in my Social Work class when I made a quick stop by my ex-husbands house to pick up something I had left. One conversation led to another and then an argument—guess what? I missed that test and got a C in the class because I just couldn't walk away and take care of me.

A.D., Utah

I take care of all the finances. My significant other enjoys a few beers at night and smokes 2-packs of cigarettes a day. I always allow room for these things in the budget and forget to allow for some TLC for me such as a spa pedicure.

T.T., California

My husband and I were talking about Halloween and costumes. I mentioned that I was going to piece together a cave woman costume. My husband responded with "will that even be sexy". Out the door with that idea-a devil costume hangs in the closet now.

A.D., Utah

I have to admit, there was not one thing about me, that I did change for him with the hope that he would just love me.

M.M., Wyoming

I go to work when I am sick.

R.M., Utah

The other evening, my husband, our good friend and I were standing in the kitchen laughing and chatting. Our friend looked at me and said, I bet you couldn't go a week without sharing intimate thoughts with your girlfriends at work. Oh I bet I can, is how I responded. As the next few hours went by, I thought to myself, why did I take this bet, I enjoy those conversations with my girl friends and that is who I am!

A.D., Utah

The gals at work volunteered me to put together two baby showers and then let me know. They didn't ask, they just told me. I planned two baby showers even though I really did not want to.

S.G., Washington

One of my boyfriends told me that he likes the way that Kate Moss looks. I soon found myself with running shoes on taking mile runs daily to be as skinny as Kate even though I was at a very healthy weight to begin with.

T.D., California

I remember him saying that he prefers girls with long hair because it makes them sexy. I have not cut my hair for three years—

B.G., Utah

I have gone to a spoof comedy, just to be with someone when I would have rather been at a psychological thriller.

V.S., California

I have always loved the outdoors; walks by a stream or a hike up the mountain. Since you asked me this question, I realized I have not gone and done any of those things since I have been dating a new guy. He likes to just chill on the couch and stay in. Even though it drives me crazy, I sit there with him.

E.H., Washington

When I was married to my ex-husband, he wanted me to be more athletic and lose some weight, so I did.

C.C., Montana

We were talking about Halloween and costumes. I made mention that I was going to piece together a cave woman costume. My husband responded with "will that even be sexy". Out the door with that idea-a devil costume hangs in the closet now.

A.D., Utah

I just bought a new pair of blue jeans. I loved them and when I turned around and glanced in the mirror, I noticed how they snuggly fit on my bottom. I was hot! Later that night, my boyfriend told me he didn't like them. I have never worn them since.

S.W., Utah

I am a real go getter and very personable. Anyone spending time with me knows this. I believe in smiling and sharing my smile with others, as maybe it would make their day. Even though I did not fully stop smiling, but someone said to me once, "you smile too much". I am not sure how they meant it, but I can tell you that I think about it more now than I ever had.

J.L., Texas

It is 3:00 am, I am sound asleep when my husband calls asking me to come pick him up because he has been drinking and is far too drunk to drive. I get out of bed, slip on my slippers and give up my beauty sleep to run and grab him.

B.S., Arizona

There have been times when I will have my evening planned to just be in, read and relax. My cousin calls and wants me to head out with her somewhere. I give up my relaxation and head out with her.

D.S., Utah

This seems to happen a lot with my children. They need a ride here or there. I have other things or places I should have been. I end up running them where they want to go or pick them up from where they just were, and I am late to my plans.

H.D., Utah

I often hide an emotion I may be feeling such as anger, discouragement or sadness so another person does not hurt because I am hurting. I think I am even over accountable most of the time.

A.D., Utah

Even though these seem like such little things, they turn big. Pretty soon, you are letting other people choose the panties you will be wearing for the day, month or year.

REMEMBER TO CREATE YOUR PANTIES FOR YOU!

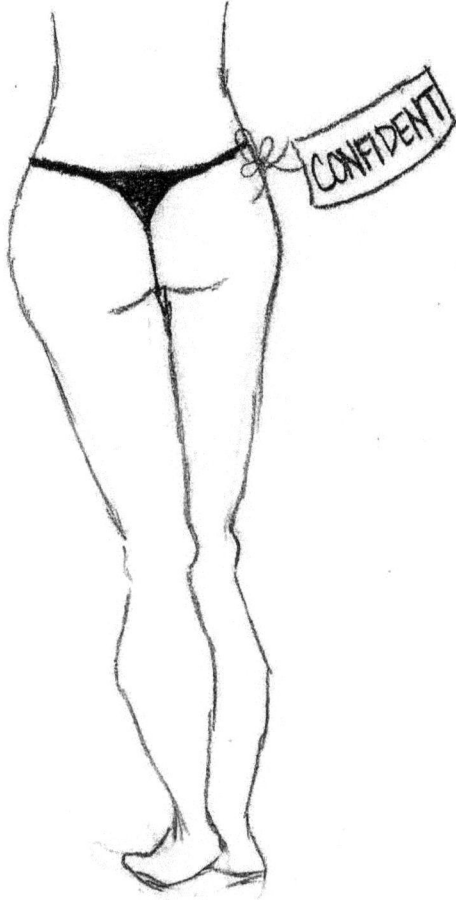

Asking for What You Want

...and the moment came when the risk to remain confined in another's pair of panties was way more painful than the risk to ask for what YOU want...

Who'd You Put Your Panties on For Today?

Asking for what you want

For those of us who have made it a habit or an addiction to please others, asking for what we want for ourselves is a very difficult and uncomfortable task. Most of us are so accustomed to putting our panties on for everyone else that we have forgotten how to ask for what we want.

It takes courage and commitment to yourself to trust that you, too, can acquire what you would like to have.

Take a vigorous look at what YOU want. (Remember, if you can think it, you can create it.) Ask yourself this over and over again…..

What do I want? What do I want? What do I want?

Raising the Panty Flags

One of my girlfriends was confiding in me a little bit about her story. She says she always asks for what she wants, but her husband just doesn't seem to hear her. She believes she needs something physical to draw his attention. Not sex, but something to slow him down so he will listen to her.

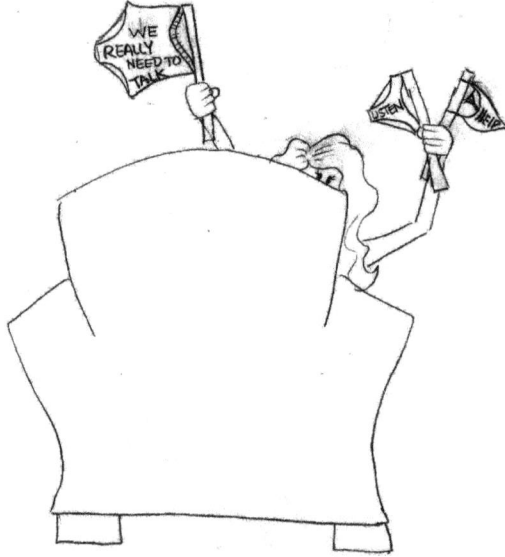

Picture this; let's say you are an individual who has a hard time asking for what you want. You have a little chat with your significant other and say, I have an idea I want to share with you and would like your support with….

When we are communicating and I am having a difficult time telling you my wants or I feel like you are not hearing me, I am going to make some panty flags. They will be attached to (fill in the blank using whatever works for you) and I will write on them what I am wanting. This in return, will allow you, my loving spouse, to step back and say, "okay. She is asking for this."

Most of us have specific areas or issues we are missing in our communication with our significant other. You could make two or three panty flags labeled, "I NEED SOME ASSISTANCE NOW", "RESPECT" and "I JUST WANT TO BE HELD FOR A MINUTE". Decide which words will work for your relationship. You could even write on the panties with a sharpie. When one of the designated situations arises, raise the PANTY FLAG!

Remember to use the "I" word when asking for "YOU" things

Since the people in your life will not be used to you asking for what you desire or that you are now taking care of yourself and expressing how you feel, you will want to be as gentle and articulate as possible.

Here are a couple of ideas to assist you to be effective when you are on your revolutionary quest for the panties you desire:

P: Problem (identify)
A: Ask
N: Negotiate
T: Thankful
I: "I" statements
E: Express

It is possible you may need to switch the ideas around a little to work for you.....Go for it. Making things work for you is part of the process of asking.

You have to get there somehow; now is a great time to start taking care of YOU by asking for what YOU want. How will anyone know if you don't ask?

Panty Insights about Asking for What You Want

For me, my conflict for asking for what I want comes when I need help around the house. Even though I work a full time job, as well as pick up a little bit of typing work on the side and go to college, I am still a full time mom and a wife, as well as a woman. For whatever reason, I have it ingrained in my head that no matter how many different things in life I am doing, I should be able to keep up with it all.

When I realized that I was taking it out on others in my family because I was not willing to ask for help, it became clear that if I did not want to do it all myself, then it was time to ask for 110% from everyone that laid their head to rest under our same roof.

It is such a peaceful feeling to walk in to a clean kitchen when I get home from work. Even though it was hard for me initially, it was so worth it and keeps getting easier.

J.F., Arizona

Well, I'm writing to first thank you for all the love and support of my photography business over the years. I really appreciate it and couldn't have done it without you. I am now going into my 5th year of doing photography and with just one (well less than one) year away from having both kids in school FULL TIME (holy cow, can you BELIEVE that?!!), I am really excited to see my business grow when I have more time to put into it!

Right now, with everyone wanting fall/holiday pictures, it can become overwhelming trying to do client sessions, last minutes holiday session for friends/family and be a mom all at once. And at the beginning of the New Year, I plan on really marketing myself so I have a steady stream of clients by the time my kids are both in school!

So please understand that due to the limited amount of time I have available I will not be able to do family/friend sessions free of charge any more. I've LOVED being able to take pictures for you all, and I'm sure you understand that a lot of my time goes into sessions/proofing/uploading/ordering/etc. BUT, I do love and appreciate all of you so I'm still going to take care of you!!! Going forward, if you would like to schedule a session with me, you will receive 50% off all session and print fees! (unless you are one of the people that I've talked to about getting pictures taken, don't worry! I'll get your session/prints free/at cost). This way I know that my time and work is valued, but you are still getting an AWESOME deal!

M.D., Utah

I finally put my panties on for myself this morning and hired a writing coach, publisher and editor. It is so fascinating when you ask something of the Universe and with faith, it provides it.

Even with the books I have read about writing and all that I had already written, my panties would really get stuck when I tried to organize it all. I had the "Am I Doing It Right?" panties on. I would get so stuck that I would actually just stop writing altogether. Now that I have Karen on board, she will be the one in charge of helping me with that. She actually had me write; I AM ALWAYS DOING IT RIGHT. Now that I think about it that is something I could name my panties for when I am struggling with the way I am writing!

A.D., Utah

I work at a facility where there are several people within a department. I have one manager; her and I have been working together for quite some time and know the ropes really well. We just hired two other gals and even though they are great so far, we would not be able to leave them on their own just yet.

My manager has been having hip problems and decided that she would ask for what she wanted, and that was to get rid of some of the intense pain she is having by undergoing hip surgery. Well, this also means that she will be out for over six weeks.

When she told me, I just sat wide eyed and thought of what it meant to me with her being gone such a long amount of time....that, I, because I had been here the longest, would be the one to take on her responsibilities. I am also an individual that would rather just take on the task myself than rely on someone to do it.

As my gut was wrenching inside, I just knew that there was no way I could do six weeks of work all by myself and I would have the opportunity to ask for some help when I needed it so I could stay away from feeling overwhelmed..

So, I did. I expressed myself, my concerns and then asked for what I thought I would need during the time she would be gone.

Whew, I feel like the next little bit will be manageable.

H.S., Wyoming

What are YOUR
Panties Telling You?

…I have not been able to wear any panties, they are all bugging me. What could this possibly be telling me?

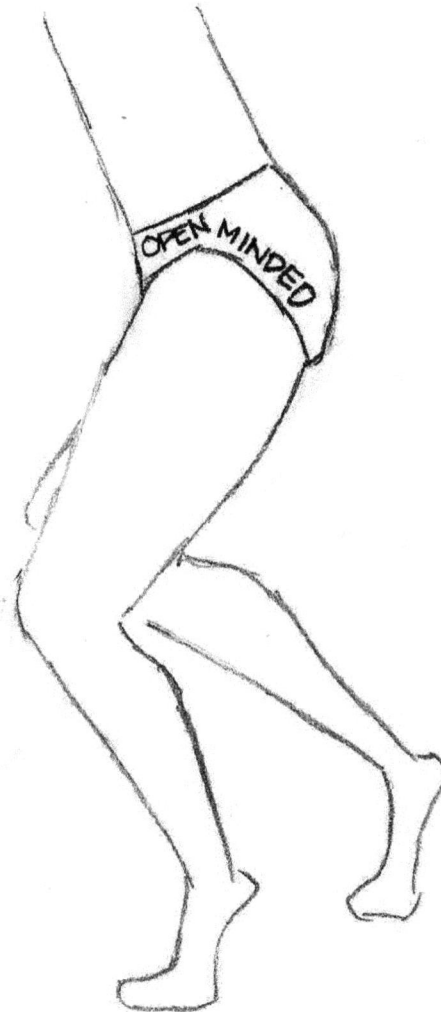

Who'd You Put Your Panties on For Today?

PANTIES IN A WAD

Getting my panties in a wad is an experience I let happen all too often. In fact, a lot more days than I would really like to fess up to, mostly on days I have forgotten who I am or what my true intentions are.

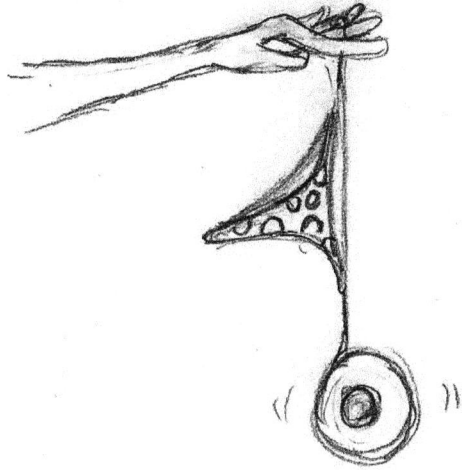

This can happen at any random split second and can be in regards to so many things; relationships, work, children, husband, best friend and sometimes even myself.

Before I know it, I find that my panties are in a wad and someone is playing yo-yo with them. I am allowing another individual to get me so upset; they have a hold of the string. Up and down, up and down my emotions go.....where I stop, is only for me to know. How long will I allow them to have power over me is completely up to me.

Oh girl, I say to myself, you are allowing your panties to be all tangled up in a big ugly wad. Time to shake them out.

I visualize sliding my panties off, shaking them out and replacing them with my black and turquoise satin hotshorts. I hold my head up high and walk on with confidence.

An Exercise Just For You

1.   *How often do you find your panties in a wad?*

2.   *What could they be representing in your life?*

3.   *What is the payoff you get for holding on to this experience?*

4.   *Are you willing to shake them out?*

5.   *What would you like to replace them with?*

6.   *What are you waiting for?   Go get it girl!*

SHARP-EDGED PANTIES

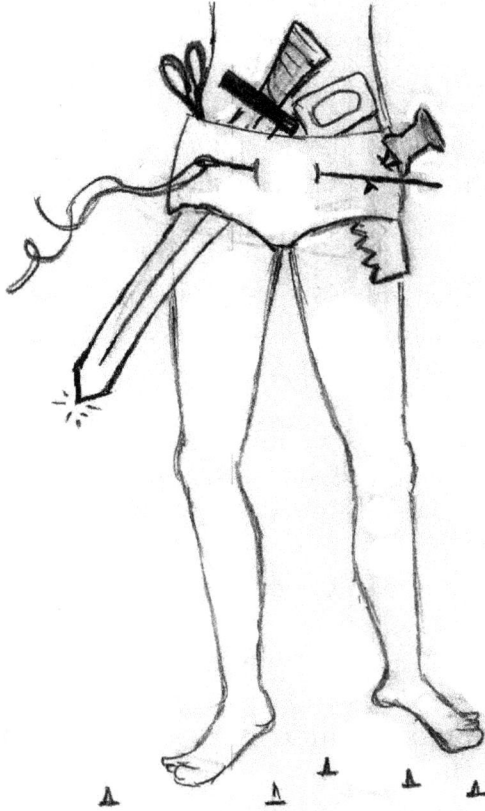

Last week I purchased five new pairs of bikini panties, striped, lacy and light colors. The elastic on the inside cuts into my inner thighs and makes it almost impossible for me to focus on anything, but sharp pain whenever I move.

 It occurred to me that I am almost finished with the first quarter of nursing school and absolutely dreading each day I am there. I am not enjoying the classes and have no interest; what so ever, in learning about chemistry and statistics. I know these classes are just generals and eventually we will get to patient care, but I have no desire to continue with schooling to become a nurse.

As I sat there, completely unfocused, my mind wandered to my favorite pair of string bikini panties that I was wearing. They are light pink with red roses, black skulls and cross bones scattered on them. The problem is, the elastic bites into the delicate skin of my inner thighs and feels like a dull hand saw is slowly and painfully cutting into my skin. This is exactly what nursing school feels like to me right now.

I remembered the question from that day in spin class, **"Who, what or why do I keep putting these panties on?"** Every day these panties are wedging deeper into my skin.

For the first time, I realized my panties were giving me reminders. I should be making a different choice, one just for me and if I didn't pay attention, the pain would simply continue and become more prominent.

I knew I was the one allowing this situation because I was worried about what people would think of me if I quit school. What about the amount of money I owe? The expense on me went deeper than just money, however.

Today, I went into the counselor's office and withdrew from school.

I came home, took those panties off and threw all five pairs away.

There is no reason to keep this situation in my life, especially since it is only causing me unnecessary pain...

An Exercise Just For You

1. *Do you have any sharp edged panties?*

2. *What could they be representing in your life?*

3. *What is the payoff you get for holding on to this experience?*

4. *Are you willing to let them go?*

5. *What would you like to replace them with?*

6. *What are you waiting for?   Go get it girl!*

THE SNUGGIE

I have one pair of panties I absolutely cannot let go of! They are part of a set, and the bra is my favorite, so I hang on to them. The weird thing is, every time I pull this pair of panties out of my drawer and dare to put them on, I spend the rest of the day pulling the material down off my left butt cheek; otherwise known as the annoying snuggie.

It totally does not make sense, I get that! What is worse is that I continue to buy more like them......I rationalize in my head, they are so cute just look at the little strings holding the front and the back together. Plus, a matching bra! I have to have them no matter what the consequences will be...I still buy them and wear them day after day, hoping something different will come of them this time---

Not so! They still ride high on the left butt cheek, keeping me constantly focused on where my panties are instead of in the present.

Why? I ask myself. Why am I not willing to get rid of the dang things already? They keep me from enjoying a well-fitted pair of panties or possibly, a well-fitted life. Is it possible I already have that, but keep reasons around to make it ever so slightly uncomfortable?

An Exercise Just For You

1. Do you have any panties that keep riding high on one side?

2. What could they be representing in your life?

3. What is the payoff you get for holding on to this experience?

4. Are you willing to let them go?

5. What would you like to replace them with?

6. What are you waiting for?   Go get it girl!

THE WEDGIE

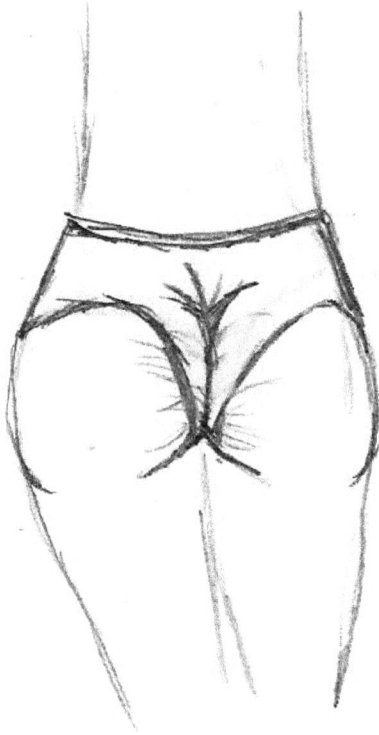

I made a comment to Goldie about how my underwear were really bugging me. He looked at me and said, "Mom, they are a reminder you should be working on your panty book." I knew he had a point and a good one.

It seems, as though, I tend to keep a couple of panties in my drawer that end up wedged right in-between my butt cheeks. When I have them on, I find myself constantly pulling and tugging at them, but the material still finds its way bunched up there over and over and over again!

The real question is why do I even keep these particular panties within reach, when I could have so many other nice, well-fitting ones? It's funny, I know, no matter how much I like how they look, the outcome will always be the same--- tugging, pulling and pushing them out of my cheeks. (I am sure someone once told me that doing the same thing over and over again and expecting a different result is the definition of insanity?).

I get stuck sometimes. Maybe this is what the ones wedged up in-between my butt cheeks represent…Movement (or lack of) and doing something to get them "unstuck" now! (other than sticking my hand down my pants when no one is looking and push them out).

Why do I even have this pair of panties on today?

Tugging at them, pulling them out……the results still remain the same!

It is obvious I am doing all the work!!! It is time to let these go and whatever it is in my life keeping them and me so deeply stuck.

An Exercise Just For You

1. *Do you have any panties that just continue to be wedged?*

2. *What could they be representing in your life?*

3. *What is the payoff you get for holding on to this experience?*

4. *Are you willing to let them go?*

5. *What would you like to replace them with?*

6. *What are you waiting for?   Go get it girl!*

CONSTRICTED

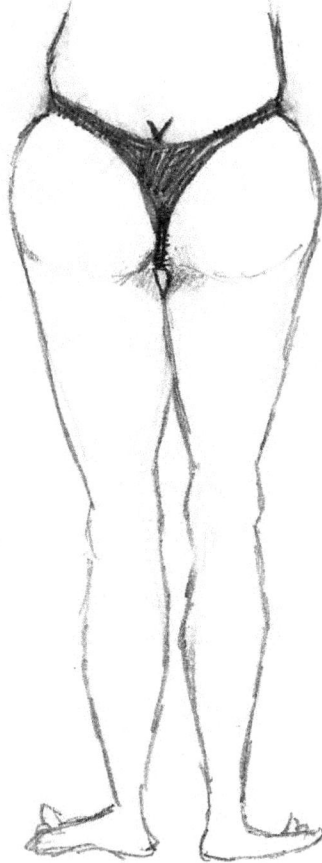

I found myself wearing one of the most constricting pair of panties one can imagine. The type gripping in on the sides of your waist, and even if you did not have a muffin top, you would when wearing these. I certainly did.

It has taken me, what feels like more than a century, to find my way out of this type of panty. I have been a very controlled individual for many years. I am one who believes if something is to get done right, I would have to do it myself. I ask others to help, but find myself going around behind them doing it my way. I created a situation where people wouldn't help me anymore because they knew I would follow behind and fix what they thought they had done an excellent job at.

The dishes were never left in the sink over night. You could not find a crumb on my kitchen floor or wipe the top of a picture frame and find remaining dust there. I covered all areas of the house. I would wipe the toilet down while sitting in a bubble bath or straighten a rug if it caught my eye while watching a favorite movie. The bed had to be made every day, which included making sure all horizontal stripes lined up perfectly.

I was the one who took care of the money because I did not dare allow someone else to do it. What if they messed something up or spent more than we had? I worked four jobs to make sure I felt secure.

I realized my body could not spend one more moment in this constricted pair of panties. They got tighter and tighter and tighter until I found myself with undue illnesses. I had to let something go…..what a blessing to rid myself of the constriction and control.

This was not an easy task for me, I must add. My mind had to be crisp and clear at all times to allow my surroundings to be a little out of sorts.

I never knew how it felt to sit and relax. Inhaling and exhaling, allowing oxygen into my body with its healing qualities; just breathe deep and cleansing breaths.

Now, I enjoy numerous sit back and relax breathing moments.

An Exercise Just For You

1. *Do you have any constricting, non breathable panties?*

2. *What could they be representing in your life?*

3. *What is the payoff you get for holding on to this experience?*

4. *Are you willing to let them go?*

5. *What would you like to replace them with?*

6. *What are you waiting for?   Go get it girl!*

THE CRACK

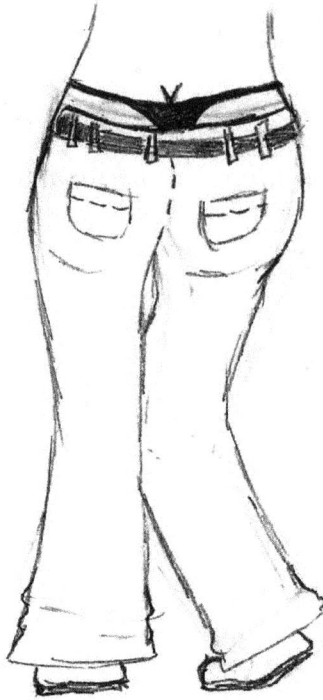

My favorite types of jeans, or shorts, typically sit on my hips and are described as "low riders". As time passes, these "low riders" seem to get lower and lower. Soon, without noticing, my jeans have dropped an inch. Not to mention, I have forgotten to accommodate for the space between my panties and the waist band, thus leaving an open and vulnerable crack for all viewers to see.

Of course, before I head to buy panties, which would fill the empty space, I continued to wear the same ones expecting a different result. However, the results remained the same. Each time I would bend over, squat down, or even sit in a chair, I was distracted by the need to pull my shirt over the back of my pants or pulling my pants up to cover up what I was letting others see; a part of me that is personal and not to be shared with just any onlooker.

I started to think of this in another way. What was I giving up of myself daily?

I headed to the store and found myself a flirty pair of hipsters. The bottoms are covered with multiple teeny tiny violet and maroon flowers and as far as the peek one would see, instead of crack--olive green lace will catch the eye.

An Exercise Just For You

1. *Do you tend to have a crack that is revealing?*

2. *What could this be representing in your life?*

3. *What is the payoff you get for holding on to this experience?*

4. *Are you willing to cover your crack?*

5. *What would you like to replace the revealing space with?*

6. *What are you waiting for?   Go get it girl!*

Who'd You Put Your Panties on For Today?

Amy Deans

Get out the Sharpie Girls

…time to label those panties…

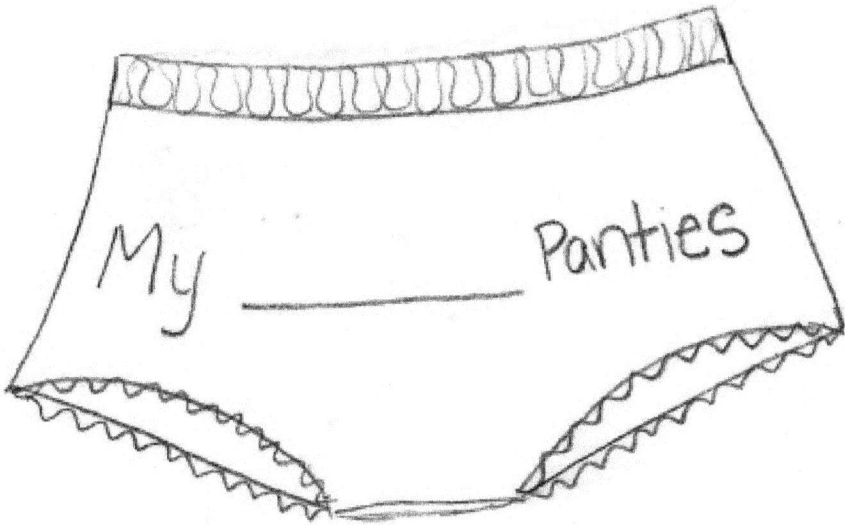

Out with the old, in with the New

Letting go of the oldie moldy panties; as well as limiting beliefs no longer fitting in your life, opens up space for new crisp and fun panties. This process allows creativity, love, joy, peace and exhilarating experiences to flow into your life.

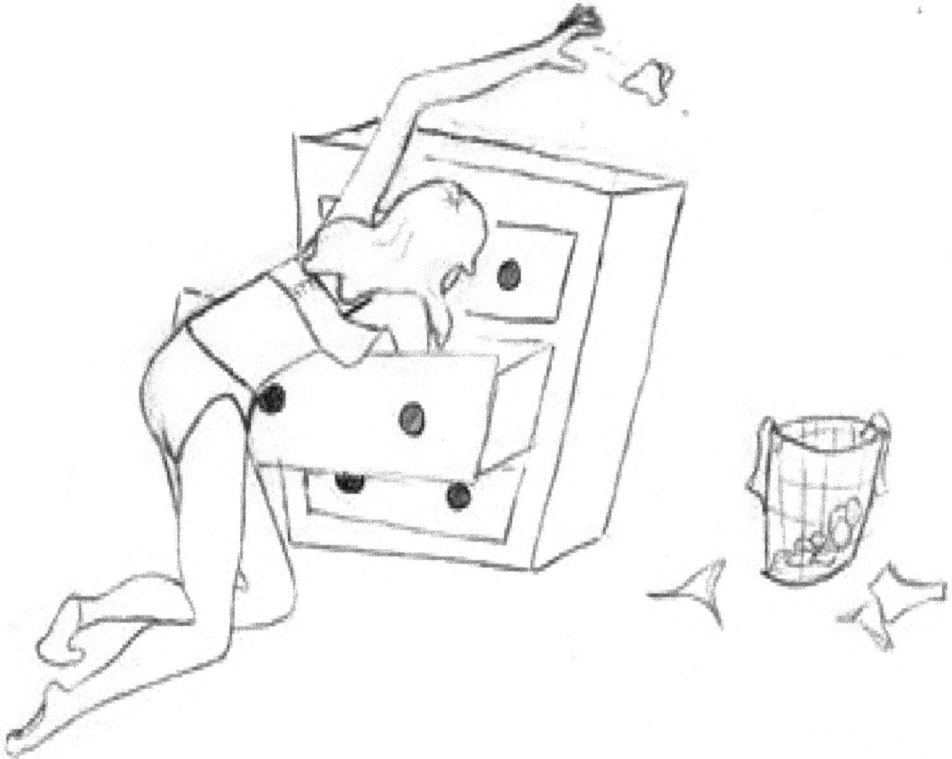

What are you willing to throw away?

Panty Discarding Insights

I even went through my bra and panty drawer and took a serious look at what I had in there. I started to clear out the older pairs to allow for newer ones or, to state it a little differently, started ridding my life of some old belief symptoms and opened up a space for new greatness to come into my life.

A.D., Utah

I found an old pair, of almost bloomers- you know, the kind that our moms thought we should be wearing as we were growing up. I just looked at them and laughed. I was still holding onto years of what I had learned from her and living that way. Well, now that I am 41, I can let those go.

S.V., Colorado

My friends did a deep panty drawer cleaning. I suggested to her that she take some of the negative things she told herself and write them on the panties she got rid of. She came back Monday and said that she actually took a sharpie and wrote things on her panties, before she threw them away.

A.D., Utah

I found myself always doing things with my friends inside when I am really an outside gal. Any of my panties that represented hiding inside and always doing what others wanted me to do; I took out of my drawers and tossed away. When I went shopping for new ones, I found Padagona briefs to be perfect fitting and ever staying in place panties. Now I head outdoors to hike and breath the mountain air as much as possible remembering that I threw away my "hide inside myself "panties.

E.M., Wyoming

For the last couple of years, I have thought about my schooling and what I want to be when I grow up. When it came down to it, I knew that becoming a nurse would be something that I would enjoy, the schedule would fit in my life perfectly, financially it was more than acceptable, I would be able to have more free time with my family and children after two years of hard work and I really wanted to do it. As I shared this with my sister in law, who has been a close advocate of mine, she said discouraging words to me, as did so many other individuals. In "MY" gut, I knew this was the choice for me....I cleaned my panty drawer of all the negative words and self defeating beliefs that filled my mind and made room for a weekly set of panties that would be comfortable for the new growth I am set out for. It will be awesome to clean my panty drawer again in two years to allow for play panties.

J.F., Arizona

I went through my panty drawer and got rid of all the panties that were just plain and simple, most of them, control top. I have always been one to make sure that everything around me was perfect because I had a fear that if I did not have control of it all, that it would fall apart, not any more, out with those panties and beliefs! I really feel like it is time to jazz it up a bit and be spontaneous; leave the dishes in the sink over night once or twice, will not be the end of my world. When I went to the store to refill my drawers, I just went with the most fun, brightest panties I could find so when I put them on, I feel like I am ready to give up some control and let go....a lot!

B.Y., Hawaii

Just within the last month, I have been on a fabulous wellness plan that took my buns to a new and smaller size. Every time I would put on a pair of my briefs, they would sag in the area of my behind. It dawned on me that I have been stuck in my past beliefs about my well being for years. After I bought several pairs of perfect fitting, silky briefs, I attached my past to those sagging bottom undies and threw them out along with any beliefs I had that were still holding me behind. It is a new feeling to be here in the present, enjoying who I am and living the way I would like to.

A.M., Utah

As I was looking through my panty drawer, I noticed pretty much everything that I had in there was skimpy and uncomfortable. I thought about how when I had bought each pair it was for the current man that I wanted to impress by being something I really wasn't. I figured that sex was love and if I could please them that way, all would be well in the relationship. Not so! I am thrilled to know that I can take all those panties and toss them out to open up for several pairs of panties just for me. The belief that someone will love me if I give them sex has now been thrown away and acceptance fills my lingerie drawers.

N.S., *Arizona*

I have always been one who has a hard time expressing myself to my loved ones. I found it hard to tell them exactly how I felt when it came to being angry, hurt, disappointed or anything in the realm of negative communication. In other words, I would not say a word or express my negative feelings to keep the peace. The downfall to all of this was I noticed I would eventually just blow like a big volcano and spurt out some of the ugliest things that you have ever heard.

I knew this was not a healthy way of communication, but I needed a push to allow myself to express how I was feeling without the fear that if I did, my loved ones would no longer love me. As I pulled out a pair of panties for the day, I realized my top drawer was filed with old, ugly panties. It was really time to get some new ones.

When I was in the panty and bra section at Target, I realized that I wanted panties that really expressed how I feel. When I got home, I took out all the oldy, moldy panties and shoved them into the garbage can. As I was doing that, I said, there will be no more hiding my feelings when they arise. I randomly put all my panties in the drawer, kind of tossing them a bit, reminding myself that when something comes up, I will express it, I will state how I feel when I feel it and, trust I will still be loved after I say it.

A.D., *Utah*

As I was growing up, when I asked for something I wanted, my dad would simply state, "poop in one hand and want in the other, and see which one you get first". Harsh, I know and that is a belief that I have had for a life time.

I really took note of that when I got into my drawers to pull out a pair of my panties for the day—I have five drawers full, of old underwear from way back when, collecting dust-bunnies. Wholly cow I thought, I have held on to all of these for years because I have believed that wanting things in my life would not happen. Oh boy, not today, I took those five drawers out to the dumpsters and disposed of them and the statement that my dad repeated to me so many times in life. I went and bought 10 brand new pairs of any type of panties that I wanted. As I placed them in my drawer, I realized that I had four more drawers of wants that I had just opened up to fill! This is fun!

J.D., North Dakota

Now I have a family, husband and pets, I put everyone's needs and wants way before my own. It became crystal clear when I was sliding my foot through the leg hole in a pair of my panties and my toes got stuck in a hole that was forming in the crotch of the panty. This was a perfect example of how I forget to take care of some of my basic needs. I riffled through the drawer to see how many other holey pairs I had stuck in there. Not to my surprise, they all had some sort of hole starting or encompassing the panty. I strung them all on a string and labeled them with the old belief that everyone else should be taken care of first and ran them out to the garbage. When I closed the lid to the garbage, I also closed the lid on that belief. When I went to buy new panties, I reminded myself that I was there just for me and replaced them with whatever panties I wanted!

K.C., Idaho

To be frankly honest with you, I have one type of panties in my drawer. There are no colors or different styles, just one type of panty. As I started to do some self investigating I learned that I have been stuck, like an animal in quick sand, just stuck in one pair and the belief that life is supposed to be hard; I have to work at it and it will never be any different than what I have known it to be. However, this week it occurred to me that I have all kinds of open ended options in my life and I want to start creating my life the way I want it to be. The first thing I did was label my plain panties with my beliefs that have kept me stuck for the last 49 years and bought me all kinds of new and move forward panties.

J.R., Nevada

An exercise for YOU

Indulge, feel and let go.

Let's get cleaning gals!

1. *Set your book aside.*

2. *Get up from where you are reading.*

3. *Move toward your panty drawer or wherever you may keep them.*

4. *Open the drawer...*

AND NOW GO FOR IT...

Go ahead throw those old panties away and when you do, write all your negative thoughts on them and let them go, too. When it comes up again remind yourself you threw your old "Belief Briefs" away.

Take a step into the new you, your own Panty Revolution.

TIME FOR A LITTLE SHOPPING GALS

You have successfully cleared your drawers of all your old panties, labeled them with beliefs no longer working for you in life and thrown them away.

Today, it is time to create new and authentic panties just for YOU!

When you are having a rough time and just can't seem to pull yourself out of it, label your panties for the day. The pair you put on for the day will be the pair you need for what comes up. (Don't know how this works, but it does and it's magical!).

You can label your panties first thing in the morning. Or if something comes up in the middle of the day, you can rename them with a new affirmation. This is a fun and enticing way to change hard times and make them enjoyable.

Go out ladies, be abundant!

Create time for your Panty Revolution.

Purchase some panties and start labeling.

There are thousands of affirmative words available, found in books, on the internet and within you. They are easy to find when you are open to the feelings being where you want them to be. But just in case you are struggling to find a few of your own, you can borrow mine for a day, two days or as long as you need.

(You can label your panties in your thoughts or if you dare, take a sharpie to them and write on them. Make it work for you.)

Positive Thought Panties

Beaming	Relaxed	Proud	Gentle
Invincible	Soft	Serene	Dynamic
Joy	Strong	Skillful	Fun
Positive	success	Valuable	Confident
Exceptional	Gorgeous	Dependable	Brilliant
Exciting	Loving	Graceful	Energized
Happy	Abundant	Breakthrough	Certain

Every Day of the Week Panties

Lighten up	Forgive/forget	I am in the present	Carefree
Open minded	Believe	Innocent	Laughter
Grateful	Worth	Love	Self Respect
Unique qualities	Integrity	Patience	Warm

Labeling Our Panty Insights

Today has been one of those days for me. Honestly, I am slow, feeling frumpy and just down right out of it. I stood in front of the mirror and tried to figure out what the problem was...couldn't figure it out...so I decided to label today's panties. It took me minute, but I stood there until I figured it out—self love.

As I was walking down the long hall towards my office at the hospital, I could feel my thighs touching and rubbing against each other with each step I took. This is just one of those experiences in my life that drives me crazy and typically, I would make a harsh statement to myself because my body is not "perfectly fit." NOT TODAY—I reminded myself that this morning I chose to label my panties "self love" and now was the time to remind myself of the feeling of self love against my skin.

I made a statement in my head. "I love, accept and appreciate the strength of my thighs and I am grateful I can walk to and from the places I need to be. This brought a grin to my lips. I am glad I chose that phrase for the day!

A.D., Utah

I want to find a pair of panties to help me remember to be spontaneous. After the feedback I have been receiving, I need to relax and let go a little bit. Maybe they could be made out of mesh for breathing room!

B.Y., California

I have had too many experiences that I can even count when I have allowed myself to be "burned" by others in my life. I feel like I have had little trust in new people that have entered my life and little confidence in me because I opened my heart and let them touch it, only to find it to be walked on. I have been walking around protecting myself by the words I am choosing to put out there. Things like, I only attract people into my life that will walk on me and disrespect me. Each time I say these things, a little twinge of pain fills my belly....I am so done walking around in these panties.

Today, I have labeled my panties so I can remind myself daily I am worthy to be loved by good people, trust and unique qualities. Now my energy is lifted and I am excited for what I can create in my life!

B.D., Washington

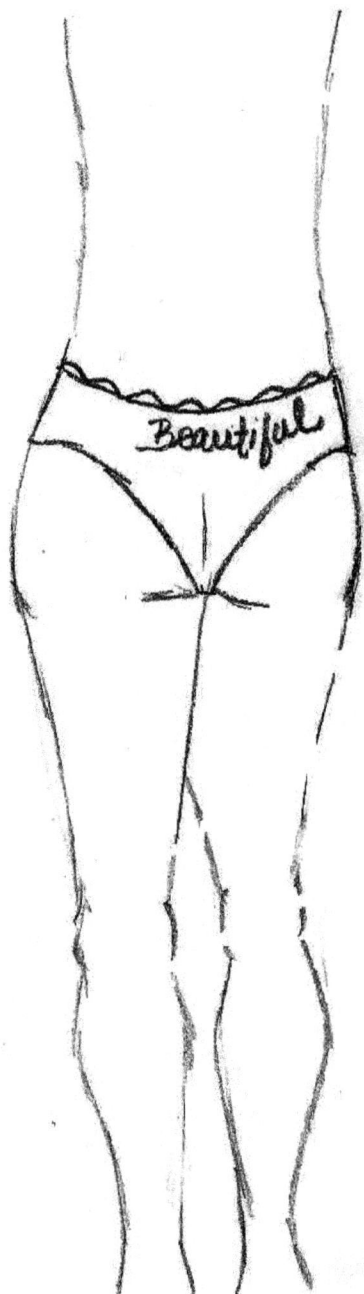

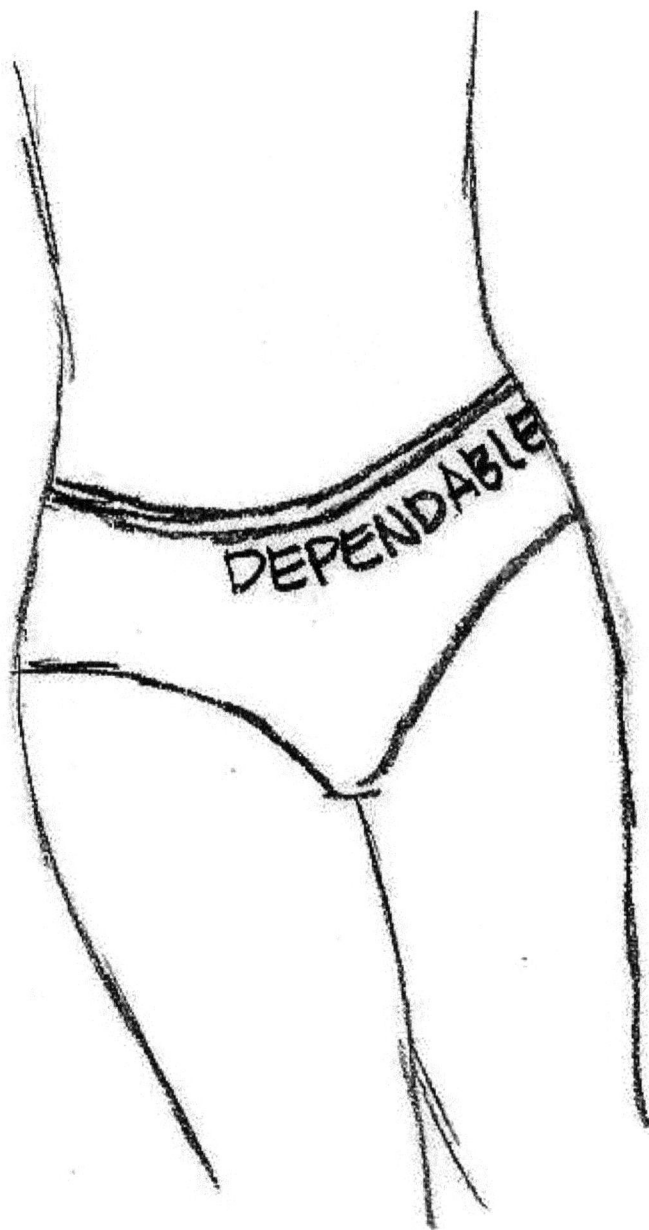

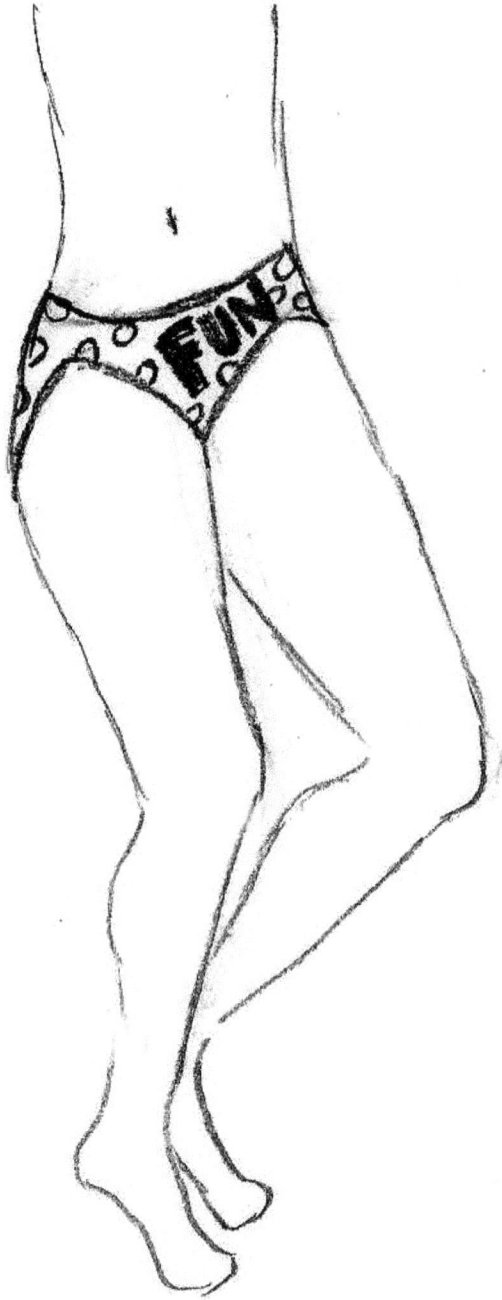

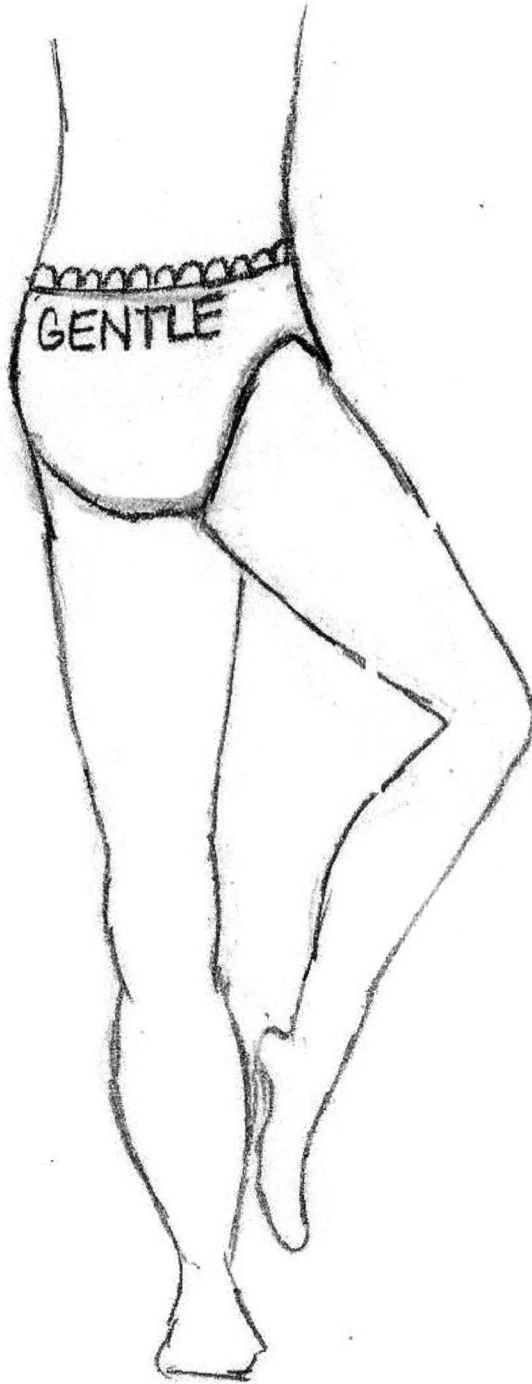

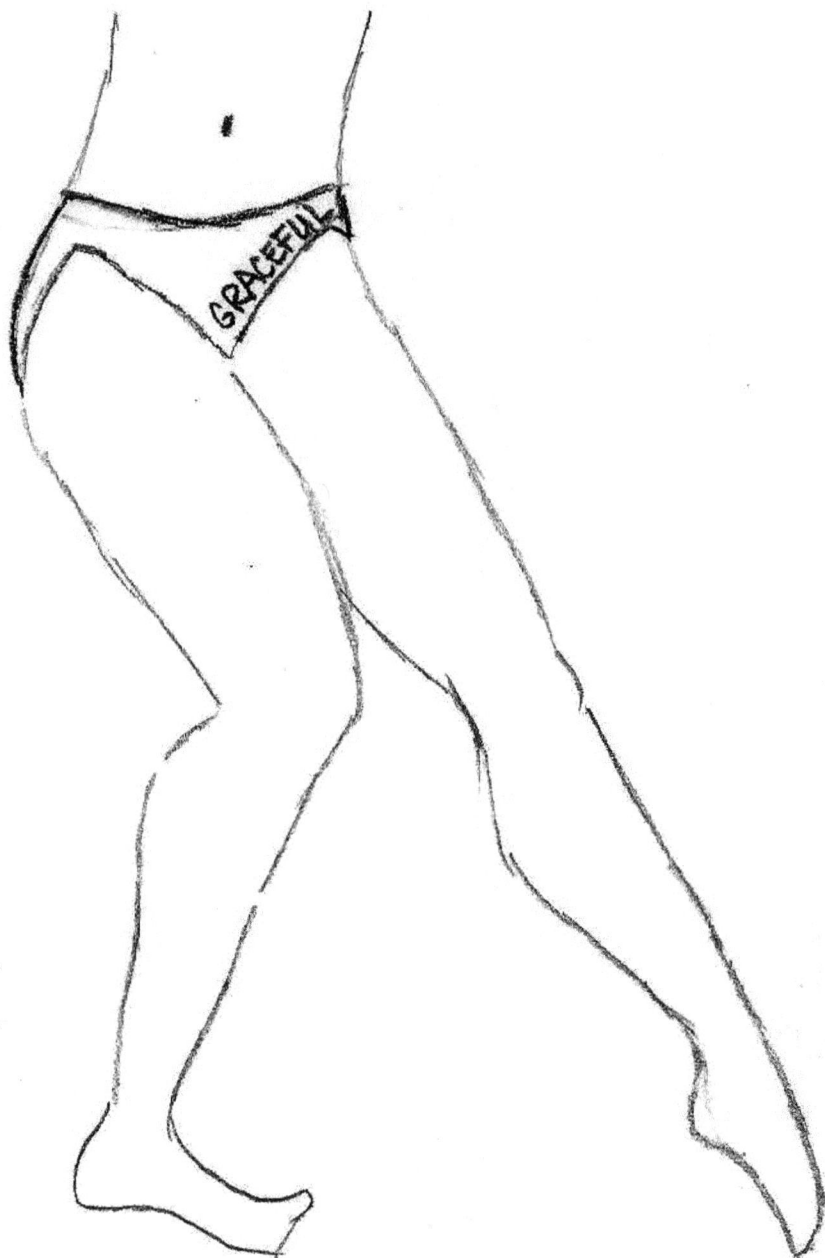

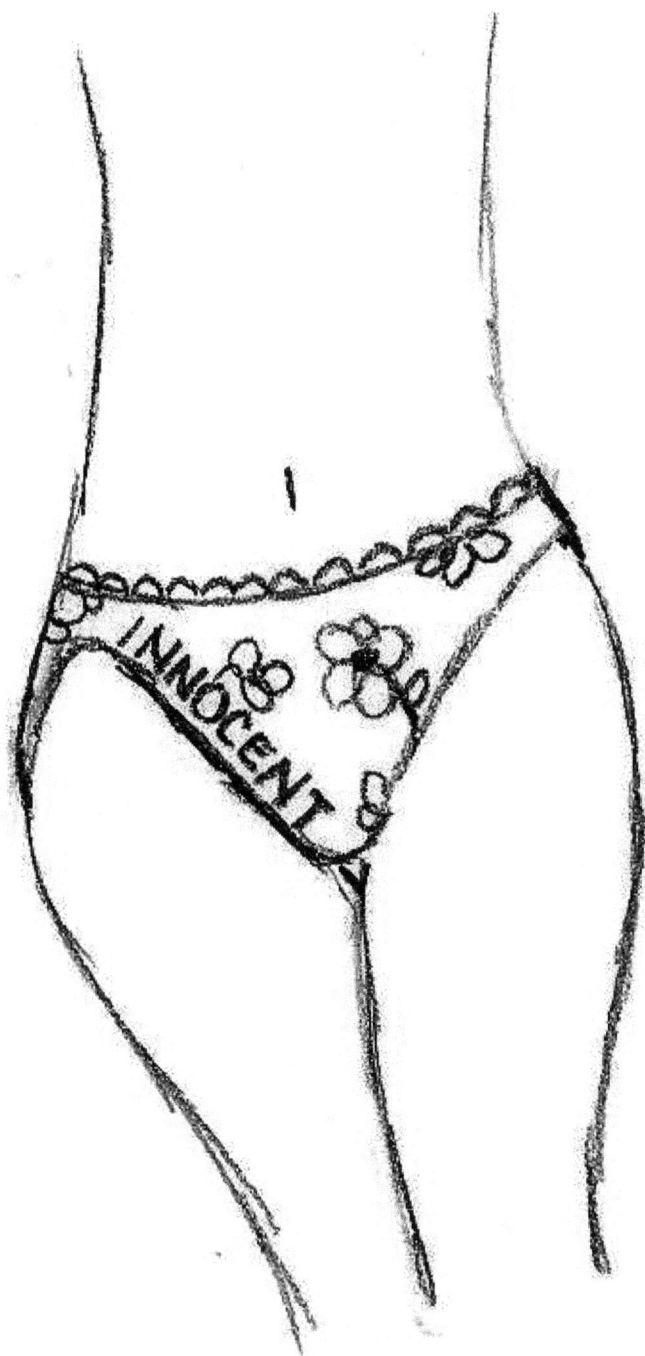

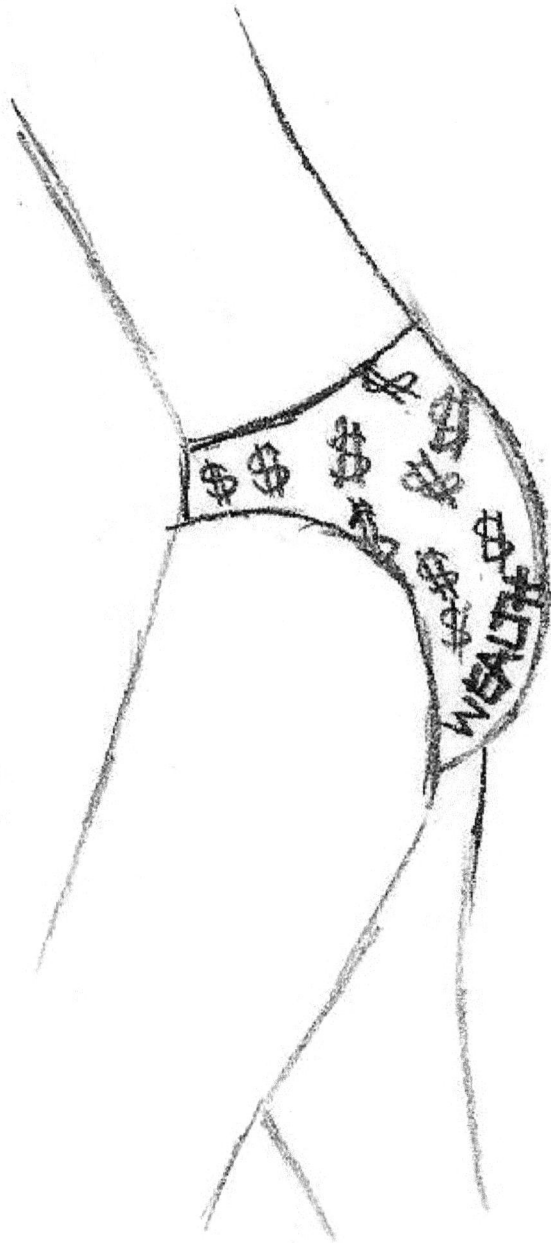

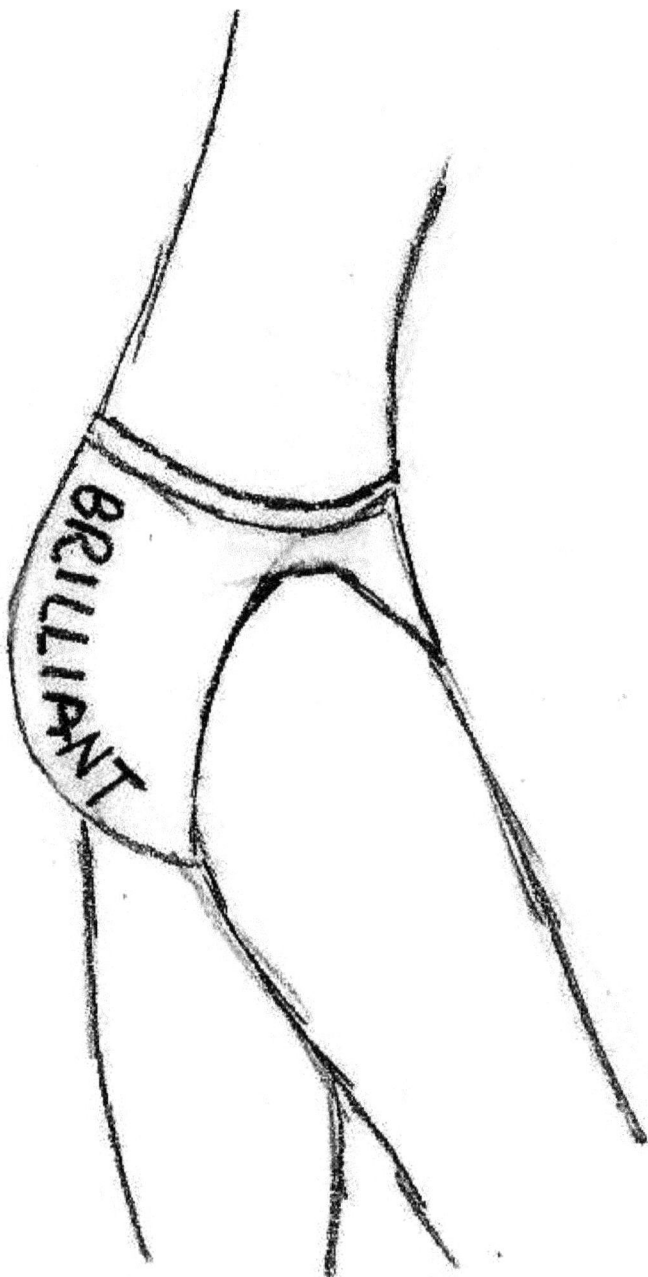

5% Spandex

…even when you think you have it all down, you will want some flexibility…

You are definitely on a progressive track now. You have thrown away your old panties, created room for new panties, have gone shopping and created YOUR very own panty revolution! WAY TO GO!

WARNING, WARNING, WARNING, WARNING, WARNING

This warning is to heed you from self-destruction and to remind you that things will still come up from time to time. THIS IS A PROCESS. It is vitally important you allow yourself some room for choices and ongoing learning experiences…..it gets easier and easier as you go…..but like most panties have some sort of spandex in them for comfort and flexibility, I ask you to allow the same flexibility in your life experiences also.

I am a master of slipping back into the role of taking care of everybody and making sure everybody is happy. Suddenly, when my back and shoulders are hunched over, experiencing tightness along with pain, I am brought back to the present and I am smacked hard in the face with the realization I have a whole lot of panties holding me down in an awkward, uncomfortable position. Some people call me the Mother of the World.

The best news about losing consciousness for a moment is exactly that, it is only for brief periods of time and YOU are now more aware when moments like these happen.

Step back, take a break, remember 5% spandex and glide on forward!

Engraved, life-long Beliefs

Belief = Something believed; a conviction or an opinion.

Interesting definition, eh? I believe this should also include "can be deadly to oneself".

I moved back home. I was excessively anxiety-ridden, more than I ever imagined I would be. As I was unpacking, my brain was stuck in the memories of the last couple of years and the struggle Jeff and I shared. Did I make the right choice? Can we be happy again? Or would we find ourselves and the relationship winding down the "this is too good to be true" path of relationship and self destruction?

Wouldn't you know it, I squatted down and my thong wedged a little further up my bottom than was comfortable. As I was pushing the little bit of material down and loose of the position, my finger created a hole in one of my all time favorite panties—zebra stripped with lavender lace around the waistband.

Later in the evening, I pondered over ideas of how I could turn this tragedy into an opportunity. I figured my lovely panties needed to go in the garbage. I had ruined them, but I wanted them to have meaning. A brilliant thought struck, I would attach my "move back home anxiety" to my zebra striped panties and throw them away. Every time a little anxiety would creep into my body or a memory of a bad time, I could simply visualize the panties in the trash and all those ugly, old, unreliable feelings with them.

I have had to do it a couple of times already. I just say to myself, "You know, Amy, you threw those away. They have been disposed of, far from you, and are no longer a part of your present relationship with Jeff.

The strangest thing happened today. I was using the bathroom, went to pull up my panties and noticed they were the same pair I know I threw away…you know the ones, zebra striped with the lavender waist band; the pair I attached all my anxiety to and threw away? I know I did! I can even see the big, black, industrial garbage can I threw them away in. I sat there dismayed, my head resting against my sweaty, clammy palms slowly shaking back and forth. What the hell?

I've been feeling anxious again. (Probably because everything is going so smooth and awesome…) I finally figured out what my "Return From the Garbage" panties are trying to tell me. There will be times these feelings, memories and old beliefs show up again, unexpected and uninvited…

After I became conscious of what I was being reminded of; once again, I removed the panties from my body, tore them in half and placed them in the wooden waste basket next to the toilet.

Unexpected feelings, thoughts and anxieties can creep back into our lives at unexpected moments, but this doesn't mean we have to hold on to them for longer than the seconds it takes to make a new choice or put on a new pair of panties that we feel secure in.

SOMETHING FOR YOU TO DO

It really works. You should try it.

Attach a belief to your panties and rid yourself of your "deadly" consequences.

There will be unexpected, undesirable moments. Allow these to be what they are.

I have had one time since Jeff and I have been back together (over a year now), when I found myself laying on the floor in the fetal position and sobbing. I can't even tell you now what I allowed to upset me so badly placing me in such a vulnerable position.

I can tell you this, it happened for a reason. I realized at that moment, that there may be times (hopefully not many more) when I didn't even think about my panties at all. I felt as if moving forward was impossible. What I did do, however, was allow the feelings to happen, to engulf and consume every bit of my being.

Just when you think you have this all down---

There will be days where nothing feels easy to you. Maybe you woke up on what you would call the "wrong" side of the bed and it happens to be a Tuesday. Everything that could go wrong, happens to you on a Tuesday—well here it is, Tuesday - can't get up, computer is slow, kids won't get out of bed and low and behold, your husband has the day off, which for some reason downright gets under your skin. Great day to change your beliefs about Tuesdays and the lack of trust gripping you in the groin area as you head off to work.

I believe as we are traveling through a new space of creating what we want and putting our panties on for ourselves, we will have moments that are rough. This is all new for us after all.

Be forgiving of yourself. Even though I did not think of my panties during this moment, enough to pull me out of the funk I was in, I was able, once I allowed my feelings and expressed myself, to put on a pair of panties reminding me that changing a life time of patterns takes time.

An Exercise Just for YOU!

1. **FEEL your panties.** *Currently, they may feel tight, gripping and smothering. But go back and start over—you can do this—you have the choice in the now, no matter what the then, even seconds ago has brought to you!*

2. **VISUALIZE** *the panties you are in RIGHT NOW*

3. **STOP!**

4. **TAKE A BREATH**

5. **FEEL WHAT YOU NEED TO FEEL** *allowing for the moment.*

6. **EXPRESS HOW YOU FEEL…"yes, I am hurt"**

WHEN YOU ARE READY AND ONLY THEN, RENAME YOUR PANTIES

Trust whatever you label your panties for the day or moment. Doing this will assist you with staying in the present and allow joy to fill your being.

Who'd You Put Your Panties on For Today?

Amy Deans

Everyday Panty Life

…progress, progress, progress…

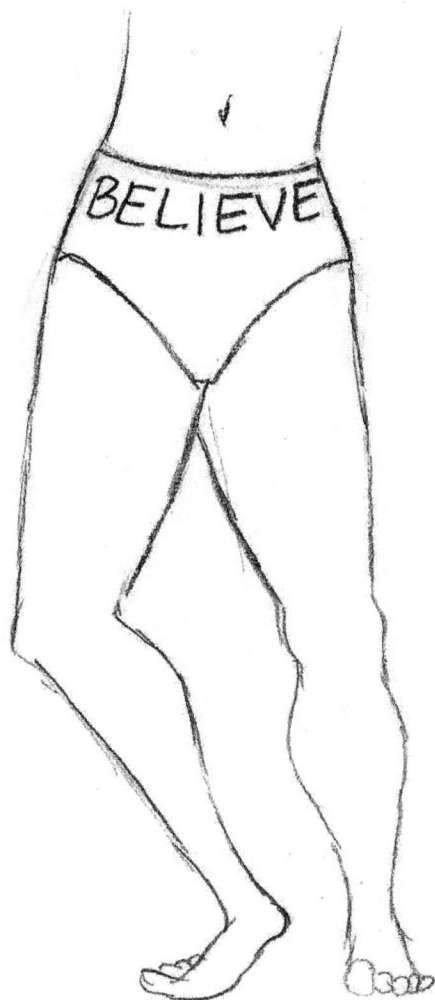

Who'd You Put Your Panties on For Today?

"Every Day Panty Life" is a collection of moments in which I have deliberately shifted my emotions, inner feelings and thoughts, creating joy in my life by labeling and truly mastering the concepts of panty awareness.

I stood at our breast-high bar in the basement. In one hand I held a sharpie, in the other, a pair of colorful, striped hip huggers. Before they were in my hand, they held space on a shelf in my closet. I never wore them, as they did not fit comfortably, just like the thoughts I was having…."I do not trust the process of life." This was evident by the vibrations that I was radiating.

I laid the panties flat on the bar, uncapped the sharpie and wrote upon them, NOT TRUSTING THE PROCESS OF LIFE AND THOSE AROUND ME in big bold letters. I was ready and willing to release this nasty belief to the universe and return to the magic of my life.

Kneeling in front of our fireplace, I wadded up several pieces of old newspaper, set the panties on top of the tower of paper and lit a corner; watching the flames engulf the thoughts I allowed to hold me in traction each time I was starting to fully enjoy my life to the capacity I knew it could be. For just a moment, my thoughts played a trick on me. I bet these panties won't burn to complete ashes, thus representing that I cannot completely let go of this stifling belief.

Too my pleasant surprise, it was time; the colorful striped panties, the black sharpie writing and my old, debilitating beliefs combined with dark smoke, floated out into the universe leaving absolutely nothing behind.

I have created a concrete visual of releasing this belief and only attracting; I DO TRUST THE PROCESS OF LIFE! I can manifest my wants in life! I am the only one who can create my joy.

Who'd You Put Your Panties on For Today?

Wednesday, June 2, 2010

Celebration Time

Just about 7 hours ago, I got word my Panty Revolution blog was up and ready to go, all I had to do was create a new yahoo email address and password, then start typing. Easy Right?

So, you ask, what took me so long to actually get going?

Well, I would say it is a combination of many emotions; excitement, anxiety, thrill, overwhelm, joy, gratitude and most of all, the sensation of knowing I am really beginning to pave a path I have only been thinking about for years; TO mY DrEAms and assisting others to become more aware of theirs.

My mind ran ramped this morning of what to say and how to say everything I would want to say and more....So I sTepped back a minute, took a breath and reminded myself there are no right and wrongs when writing and if I did not write immediately even though I had been waiting for this exact moment to move forward, it would certainly be okay.

Because this blog and my upcoming book are about WHO WE PUT OUR PANTIES ON FOR......I headed to the store for my own set of new CELEBRATION panties.

I would have thought this would be so easy--I could visualize what I wanted them to be like; a very light, airy material with bright colors and cheery-they had to be cheery, not sensual. Something just for me.

When I got to my destination, the panty and bra section in Kohl's, and what a large section it is, I found myself taking in deep breaths and slowly blowing them out. My thoughts were only focused on one thing at that time, MONEY and should I be spending such and such amount on a new set of matching bra and panties when there are two birthdays coming up, vacation, dirt bikes to be purchased for the boys, modeling pictures to cover for my daughter, graduation, exchanges of services (to some, bills) to be paid and etc, etc, etc---you name it, I am sure that there was something else or somewhere else that maybe I could have put the cash.

This is what is so important though, all those other things I mentioned above, have to do with someone else, important someone else's, yes, but it is important to celebrate our own successes--and today is one for me!

92% polyester 8% spandex Boyshorts.

The base color is white and there are bright green, pink, red and turquoise polka dots on them. The bra is matching with light pink that lines the edges and make up the straps!

I found the perfect celebration set and every time I put them on, I can promise you, the same excitement and chills currently are running through me---will return.

Thursday, June 3, 2010

5% Spandex

Earlier this week I came up with the most beautiful plan on how to fit everything I do into a 24 hour period. There were obvious things that I had to work around, like my Medical Assisting job at the hospital which is from the approximate hours of 8-5. So, this is what I came up with...

4:00 a.m. rise, get the coffee going, and work on my book.
5:30 a.m. put in an exercise tape or what have you, and work out.
6:00 a.m. walk the dogs
6:30 a.m. get in the shower and get ready for work
7:30 a.m. head out the door to work
8-5 work at the hospital

5 p.m.-whenever, spend time with the family and maybe a little bit of medical transcription depending on where all the kids are and my husband.

Weekends, -Type, do some laundry, Type, clean the house, Type, have a glass of wine, Type.

It was the perfect plan until last night, when I couldn't sleep. Soon the 4 a.m. wake time turned into hitting the snooze button until 5:45. Then I had a moment of dilemma--which task do I choose.

I picked: make coffee, write for 20 minutes and walk the dogs. As I was getting dressed, I pulled on a pair of light pink, cotton lace thong panties.

As I read the label on this pair, I thought, these have got to be cotton, and sure enough they were, but they were also 5% Spandex. It hit me.....spandex is what allows the underwear flexibility to move in perfect motion with each movement I make so they don't end up wedging up between my butt cheeks making walking completely uncomfortable.

I compared this to life, how I need to allow for flexibility without beating myself up for not completing everything that the above schedule has laid out for me. It made walking the dogs a completely different experience....I did not rush, I let them off their leashes and do their own things in their own time, I admired the mountain range and watched the sun come up and the colors in the sky change...I even remembered to breath.

All day long I listened to stories very similar to mine in one way or another of co-workers and friends...some of them talking about their diets, some about their own schedules, relationships, exercise or commitments that they had made to themselves at one time or another and have slipped......just like me. But what stands out the most is how we are all so quick to self abuse because we have not been able to meet the irrational set of expectations we put on ourselves.

So, from now on gals, remember that there is always room for 5% spandex in our lives!!! ENJOY.

Friday, June 4, 2010

Fuscia Over Body

It just happens to be Friday and my body and mind are feeling it. I am moving slowly. My body thinks that maybe my shoulders should ache today, my eyes should spontaneously close and my head might be found bobbing in a downward position, which then can lead to somewhat of an out of control spiral of not feeling so patient with people and a little on edge....

Today, I have it beat:

To the closet I head. I know exactly what set I need to get me through the day. Fuscia, bright and spontaneous!

Friday, June 4, 2010

Evening Follow Up-Fuscia Over Body

Just a little update to say my day turned out fabulous.

The aches in my shoulders and the drowsy feeling I originally had, went away. Work went by quick and I absorbed many smiles and shared many smiles.

It always amazes me how so much is connected to thought process.

Let's take a quick look...

I literally drag myself out of bed and have to think about every step I make into the kitchen as my feet feel like they each have thousand pound weights attached to them. I brew some coffee, sit down at the computer and my mouth is hanging open, spit collecting in the corner of the creases of my lips absolutely determined to make a stream of drool that will eventually splat onto the letter "N" on the keyboard. My upper eyelashes are positive that they need to meet with the bottom eyelashes and I should let my head drop right onto the keyboard just to sleep for 10 more minutes.

How in the world am I going to make it through this day? This is when the fuscia catches my eye from the arm rest of the puffy green chair sitting in front of me......I lean to the right side to catch a glimpse, and realize this is the exact set to get me through the day.

Just with that, I already started to perk up.....I grinned to myself and suddenly had visions of 365 pairs of panties and bras to choose from and label----how fun this is going to be!

Monday, June 7, 2010

Crisp, Clean and Confident

Today is a peaceful Monday morning. I simply have a little Jim Brickman piano music pulled up on Pandora (the online free radio station) and the birds are singing their early, before the sun comes up, tunes outside of the bedroom window.

I finished all weekend medical transcription, spent time with family and really had an enjoyable weekend.

I have been working on worksheets my writing coach, Karen, has put together as part of her program, "The Heart and Soul of Business". They are fantastic.... I am creating what I want my business/writing to be like from the hours I want to work, to the individuals that would consists of my clientele; who they are, where they come from, how I want to be treated by them, what they will learn from me and what I will learn from them. My ideal income. Where I will be and where I will work from and anything else that I can possibly think of.

It is so much fun and my pencil carried on and filled lines of my notebook as I drew out, without holding back, everything that I want. Not only that, but I am confident that I can create it and the stepping stones will be laid out in front of me to continue forward.

As today is Monday, early, the beginning of a new day, a new week and an opportunity to create...

I suggest, as I will also do, grab any pair of panties, put them on and remember today is a new day to create life as you want it!

Today I put on my "Start again panties"... I have decided that today really is a new day and I'm not going to get down on myself for slipping up on my recent wellness goals. I've found the pink, lace panties (including that 5% spandex) and have made the determination that TODAY IS A NEW DAY!!

A.M., Utah

Thursday, June 10, 2010

UPside DowN

Sometimes I just run into one of those days in life....Even though my feet touched the ground out of bed in the morning with gratitude and excitement for a new day, it seemed maybe outside forces were going to see how far I could be pushed.

It started little. I was printing some finished transcription letters. Going along happily, letter 10 now printing; I gazed over at the printer and something did not look quite right. The past 10 letters were printed UpsiDe DowN on the letterhead. I giggled to myself and flipped the paper and started to reprint. No big deal was the thought I had at the moment and returned to printing from there....it only gets better though; pretty soon it seemed like something besides myself was controlling what was happening around me...

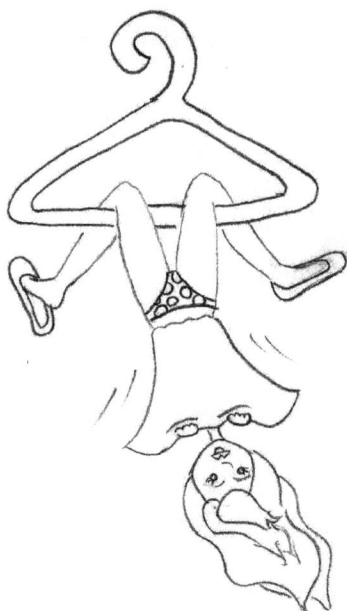

The computer slowed way down making it so each time I would transfer between applications, I would see a white screen for about two minutes....two minutes really starts to add up when you are trying to get things done...next Pandora freezes and the music that relaxes me first thing in the morning has turned to silence....

I'm still okay, but now starting to wonder if this is any indication to how the rest of the day is going to be? No biggy, I can walk away from a slow computer and finish up what I am doing later, I have created flexibility in my life....

Out to the Bronco I head.....but I can't get in, all the doors are locked and for whatever reason, we can not put a key in and unlock them. The automatic door opener has a dead battery or something. I pound it on the back of my hand because that typically works; throw it on the ground because that has worked in the past as well, not this time. As my last resort, I roll down the back window, and start climbing through to the front seat......and I was in a skirt.

I grab the garage door opener and push down hard on the little button in the middle, nothing happens, it just won't shut and each time it starts to, it freezes about half an inch down from where it originally started. So I push on the button again, and it goes back up.

Up and half an inch down, over and over again. Now those doors on the bronco I could not originally open, are wide open as I hop out and enter the code on the side of the garage to get it to close....SERIOUSLY!

A dull headache is creeping up between my shoulder blades and gripping the sides of my temples.

I could honestly go on and on about the little mishaps of the day. I even created new lyrics to one of my favorite songs by Diana Ross....

Upside down, **world** you're turning me.

Inside out and round and round.

However, all in all it really was a perfect day. It brought to my awareness there are days even though I may have labeled my panties one thing in the morning, as the day moves forward, I may need to re-label them something else to keep my spirits up and glide onward.

Just because my day started upSiDe down, certainly did not mean I had to keep it that way!

Monday, June 14, 2010

tHE PerFEct FiT

I know it may surprise you, but the bra and panty set I bought to celebrate my blog; the bra does not fit. It is too tight and smothering around my chest and if i did not know better, I would think if I was not careful, my breasts may at any unsuspecting moment, pop out from behind the padding holding it all in, in the first place. This may work for some but not me, I have come to find there are way too many choices out there, to stick with something that does not fit right.

So many of us seem to hang on to things that do not fit us. We are moving and twisting and pushing and pulling to try to get it, whatever it is, to better fit in our life. However, the result is always the same....you continue to do all the work and hope out of some miracle you will wake up and today, what does not fit, WILL.

You may see this in a relationship, a "so called friendship", your job, all you try to fit into one day, a certain workout, a diet, a new romance or an old romance, a favorite pair of panties or even a celebration bra! What ever the circumstances are, I am here to tell you, you do not have to hold on to one thing and make it work if it is uncomfortable for you. Pretty soon you get angry and resentful.

This, of course, does not happen in a blink of an eye, I totally understand, as I continued to *try* to make my new bra fit me...after all, it was part of my set and represented a momentous step forward in my life...it may take a moment for you as well.

Whatever the circumstance may be, letting go could free you to move forward to new beginnings and something bigger, fitting you better. It may take you several attempts and possibly even criticism from those around you but as you do this, always keep in mind that you will get there and the time you arrive will be just the progress you want.

P.S. I have found the perfect place for a bra that won't fit, in most cases it would be a garbage can! However, in this case, it will be framed with my celebration panties along with the words from my first blog...so I can still celebrate my success!

Letting go of what no longer fits is allowing more to flow into your life! After my recent change in size, it has been a challenge to let go of some favorite clothes that are just too baggie to wear! I put the shopping off as long as I could ....then when I finally found some clothes that fit my new image I felt so excited I immediately emptied my closet of all the OLD stuff! WOW it felt empowering! My first purchase was a dozen pair of "panties"! I love this!

D.O. Utah

Wednesday, June 16, 2010

Pant-EASE

I have to say ever since I have had this blog up and going, I have pretty much been eating, drinking and sleeping all different types of panties, colors, what they mean and what they can represent. My mind is exploding with ideas and when I can't sleep due to over thinking of what to write next, instead of counting sheep, I count white cotton briefs hanging from a clothes line and swaying softly in the breeze.

The reason I share this is because my nature has been to take care of others before myself. I have only really learned throughout the last couple of years why I do this, what the payoff is and if I don't choose to put myself first, I would be full of resentment for others over the choices I make.

My mind even went a little backward when I started blogging....I thought, how am I going to keep up with this Monday thru Sunday along with everything else I do throughout the week--I already get up at 4:00 am to make my current silver plate load work, 3:30 is just too early.

So I decided just like all things in my life, there is a balance that would also have to take place with blogging and I created a new type of Panties; Pant-EASE. Being able to be at EASE with when, how much and how creative the blog is and it will be just perfect.

EASE on forward ladies, it is much more fulfilling.

Tuesday, July 6, 2010

Lake Powell 2010

With 10 adults and 8 children plus another family of 14 and yet another family of 8 passing through for part of the trip--LAke PoweLL 2010 was absolutely a delight and also a reminder to me that even though you may be in a swim suit rather than your favorite pair of panties, it is just as easy to get them all in a wad if you so allow.

It happened to me only once this trip--I was wearing the "I like to do it my way swim suit". Mom and I were in charge of meals for the day--at home, I am very organized when it comes to meal times, as I have seen that with 3 teenagers and 1 young man on his way to being a teenager, that if I let loose and say dinner is ready, that is it, the food is gone, skull candy is still plugged into ears, and somehow the cell phones have become an integral permanent appendage to their bodies....and what used to be known as family time, has now become, all for them self time.

Mom is not quite used to this anymore and before I knew it, I had 18 people standing within a 5 foot range of me in the houseboat kitchen ready to eat.......whoa did my swimsuit get into one of the biggest wads I have ever had before....not pleasant for me or those around me.

I tell this story, because it is easy to do and it happens every day.....we get ourselves and our emotions all up in arms about some of the little things that could simply be changed with some nice words and asking for what it is we want at that exact moment in time....rather than taking our anxieties out on those we love around us.

It took me moment to realize that getting so worked up over something so little could have easily been prevented. It is always good to be aware and to be able to make a change, maybe it was not right then, but guess what----I was aware so that next time, I have the pair of "I like to do it my way swim suit or panties on, I can remember that they are incredibly uncomfortable all bunched up and stuck!!!

Shake it out gals and be willing to learn from the moment!

Thursday, July 8, 2010

Panties over There!

Yes, I know this sounds kind of fun and exciting, panties over there! Where? Exactly! What are your panties doing over there?

Let me tell you what is on my mind. Self WORTH!

According to the Webster dictionary, here are some of the definitions I came up with that involve this word in various forms.....

-The sense of one's own value or worth as a person; self-esteem
-Honorable; admirable.
-Deserving
-The quality that renders something desirable, useful, or valuable
-Quality that commands esteem or respect

If you read and re-read the powerful words above, you will take note; **no where does it say it is the responsibility of another to change their life to make you feel your own self worth.**

I am not sure why this seems to happen to so many of us. We all come from different, yet very similar backgrounds and so I do not think there is just one clear explanation as to why we have a tendency to place our *self-worth panties* in the hand of another.

This can take the shape of many different scenarios: placing your life on hold to fit into theirs, waiting for someone to put the bottle down and put you first, if only so and so would change such and such, that would tell me that he/she really does love me.

Oh what a scary thought process that eventually will only lead you one way---Dooowwwwwn to anger and resentment.

However, this is perfect....if you have come this far and you can see you are placing your self-worth in the hands of another, you are on your way to either getting your *self-worth panties* back and on your body or letting go and creating a whole new pair.

In the meantime, be forgiving of yourself and remember the only person providing your worth-----is YOU.

Put on your "I am WORTHY" panties and start creating YOUR desires.

I have read and re-read this blog over and over...In reading it, I realize my self worth IS indeed OVER THERE... in the hands of others. Thank you for pointing this out to me. I will choose myself and know that having a "SELF" is more important than having a relationship. Love you!

S.V., Colorado

Monday, July 12, 2010

Slow it down Panties

Typically I am a woman who will start the day even before I get out of bed. With the first hit of the snooze button, my mind is already on a rampage of all I should get done that day. When I finally get up, the first touch of my toes on the gray carpet of my bedroom floor is done with the full on ambition to get everything done that I have packed into one 18 hour day.

This past weekend, I challenged myself to slow down...I noticed as I was pouring my coffee with my right hand, my left hand was scrubbing the kitchen sink. WOW, I thought to myself and started the SLOW it DOWN panties challenge.

I took my cup of coffee and headed to the back deck and the sunshine. It took a real conscious effort to just sit and enjoy the present moment. I have to tell you, it was tough for me. As I sat there for the next however long it was, I observed myself...I took note sitting still was making me incredibly anxious. My leg would bounce up and down and I continued to watch for the appearance of blue ceramic beneath the coffee, telling me I was soon coming to the end of my first cup and I could get moving.

I thought about how I typically drink a cup of coffee. I take the cup with me to the computer, and then into the bathroom to get ready for work. I take the cup with me wherever I go and realized I really never stop long enough to actually enjoy what I am ultimately starting my day with and I rarely have much more than 2 or 3 swallows of it.

It took time to master this enjoyment of not doing. Every time I would get anxious to get moving, I would remind myself to SLOW it DOWN girl and enjoy what was around me...the flight and chatter of the morning swallows, the 100 year old maple tree and the warmth of the sun gently covering my whole body. Even though it took a lot of thinking, evaluating and self intent in the beginning, it was amazing what it brought to the rest of my day....I felt relaxed, enjoyed my family more, was at ease inside and nothing was more important than just enjoying every moment in the moment it happened.

If you are one of those constantly moving women---reach for your SLOW it DOWN Panties and enjoy the moments.

Thursday, July 15, 2010

Just Enough

Today is one of those days I put on a pair of black cotton boyshorts with red lace trimming the outer part of the material and a little tiny red heart embroidered on the right, top side!!! one of my favorite pair, no doubt.

But today, not so, they are riding high on my left butt cheek just enough to cause me enough irritation for a day in clinic.

This uprising, so to speak, was not at all sudden either. It happened the minute I got out of the car this morning and was walking into the building...I just tried to ignore it for the moment and when hitting the platform between flights of stairs, I snuck my hand down the back of my scrubs for a quick, left side un-wedging and headed back to the next flight of stairs. This typically will resolve the problem with this particular pair of panties, but not today-- for some reason, the sneaky things just keep crawling up on one side.

It was time to ask the question... What are my panties trying to let me know for the day? Two thoughts came to mind—

1. Is it time to rid myself of something old and create room for new things? Hmmmm possibly. (and always a good idea), OR...

2. Am I holding on to a feeling not benefiting me and my intentions of love and joy in my life?

Bingo! Number 2 wins.

The last couple of weeks, even though for the most part life has been care free, we have been having our first experience of teenagism, and I am not so much enjoying it.

I am sure this is what the little riding high nudge is for. I have hung onto the feeling making my stomach churn long enough for it to produce appropriate discipline and it is now time to let it go.

Thanks for the insight panties!!!! I am moving forward now.

Tuesday, July 20, 2010

pRogreSS not PeRfecTioN

As I was looking for a little something to add to this blog, I found Tinkerbelle stuck in a key hole. Although you cannot click on her and see what happens on the other side, I can tell you she is having a hard time getting the bottom half of her body all the way through the hole to achieve a sense of freedom. Her little bottom just will not fit and her legs are kicking in and out trying to manipulate an extra push to discharge her from the situation she has gotten herself in to!!!

Does this at all sound familiar to you? I know it does for me. I also realized, as I am writing this, when I want every single thing in life to be perfect:

-without errors, flaws, or faults
- complete and whole
- excellent or ideal in every way

I also get stuck....

These are the little things that seem to push me over the edge...dog hair on the floor, unmade bed, fingerprints on the counter top and refrigerator, I have even been known to get out of the tub and clean the toilet...No wonder why I feel overwhelmed at times.

Yesterday, when I got home, this is exactly how I felt and today, I know exactly why....I was focused on perfection rather than progress.

My writing coach asked me write on a 4 X 5 card, to carry with me always.....

What is the worse thing that could happen if I don't get it done?

Great question!

Today-I labeled my panties, PRogress, forget the perfection!

Thursday, July 22, 2010

Surrender!

My x-husband use to always say, "Some days are better than others."

I would say most days are here so we can learn from them....Today was one of those days for me.

When I am not writing, doing medical transcription, being a mom or a wife, I am a Medical Assistant in the Liver/Kidney/Pancreas Transplant Clinic. I would say that the majority of the time, I really enjoy my employment there, the interaction with those individuals that come into clinic and what I call the "Women Council", that is all the gals I work with in the front office.

Today was different though; even though I appreciate all the good and a second chance at life that comes from an organ transplant, I also see so much pain and sickness along the way, and sometimes death. More than once, I have heard that people in the health care industry have a *special gift* that they can take care of others, so I think for most of us we stay strong for those around us that are so ill with the hope that we can offer some light.

I met a melting point this afternoon. I usually can hold everything together and no one would ever know anything was bothering me, especially in a work setting.

When I got in the car to come home, I sobbed and continued for a good part of the remainder of the afternoon. I did my best to figure out what exactly was bothering me and I am not sure I really even have an answer that is clear enough to jot down.

What I do know, however, is that there will be days when life throws you a curve so you can learn from it, no matter how many panties you have in your closet.

Lesson Learned: Being strong can also mean surrendering before you bottom out!!!!

Friday, July 30, 2010

Choice

This week has been an exciting week for me.

I have made a long awaited choice and have really started to believe in myself and my upcoming creativity.

For the next three weeks, I have created a space for me to focus solely on The Panty Revolution, as well as Who'd You put Your Panties on for this Morning. I am really excited to be moving forward and to being open to more creativity!

I had a little bit of a health issue that caught me off guard, but I am back now and full steam ahead.

Remember to make choices and create space for what it is you want in life. It is possible!

Monday, August 2, 2010

Basic Cotton and Comfort

Welcome to August!

Since my little health experience last week, I have been taking it easy and resting as much as possible, and my body would not let me do much differently.

I had my mind set on getting up and getting back to routine today. It did not quite work that way however.

Last night before bed, I asked the Universe to give me a hand with creativity but I forgot to ask for specifics, such as....when I sit down to write. Instead, my mind was full of ideas all night long and I did not sleep too well. Finally, about 3:30, when I wanted to be getting up in a half hour at 4:00, I fell asleep. Well, that threw me off and I got up at 6:00 instead. Good thing I have 5% spandex in my life! So I can be forgiving of myself.

The whole morning actually fell right in line....I put on a dress, didn't so much like it! Changed into dress pants and a cute sweater; didn't like those either. Put a bunch of little ringlets in my hair and didn't care for the Shirley Temple look either....I finally went for scrubs, a T-shirt and pulled up my hair, all comfort. The only thing that could have made it better would be flip-flops but close to bare feet is not so professional when you work in a medical office, so I went for my Vans and YES, I have gone with the very basic, white, cotton, coziest pair of bra and panties that I have...I feel great!

I have a feeling I may have to refer back to this day quite a bit to remind me comfort and relaxation are soooooooo very important when registering 4 children for school, buying them each a couple of new outfits, school starting for me, writing and creating, a mini vacation with Jeff, the Texas Uprising, work, my little sisters birthday and enjoying daily life.....Whew!

If you don't have your own set of comfy, cozy panties, head out and get you some....

Remember we all need days of Relaxation.

Wednesday, August 4, 2010

a Trip to the LoT

Finally, after much planning and making sure all girls from the Woman's Council, those of us working together in the front office, were available and free on Saturday the 31st, a girls night was planned.

We would meet at my house; make pasta, garlic bread and a green salad along with something sweet to top it all off. Fill our glasses with wine and sit downstairs in front of a big screen and watch *Under the Tuscan Sun*--a real chick flick from what I understand, and enjoy each others company away from a work setting. We would top it off by chatting throughout the night and sitting in the hot tub.

I asked my husband over a month ago if he would take the kids and go spend some time at Brian's so I wouldn't have to worry about being the care provider for anyone that night but myself. He agreed and they, Jeff and Brian, decided they would take the kids camping for the night up to Brian's lot in Fruitland, Utah.

As life would so have it, one gals children were sick, another one went into labor during the day and throughout the night, and another; her grandma had a heart attack and she went to see her in Logan. For many good reasons, our girl's night was canceled.

Jeff, of course, invited me up to the lot but I declined and decided rushing to get everything else done I was committed to for the weekend; going just was not going to work for me.

At first I had some real mixed feelings about declining. I had always wanted to go, as I had never been there, I really enjoyed camping and truthfully, it is sometimes hard for me to say NO, for some irrational fear that someone might take that the wrong way but I stuck to my decision and planned my weekend accordingly.

As they loaded up 3 of our children and Brian's 2, plus all the gear, food, drinks and the two of them, I was so relieved that I decided to stay behind. I had an ear to ear smile as they drove out of the driveway. I waved and was pleased with myself---**way to put your panties on for you Aim** and let them be in charge of the kids for a weekend.

I hear this so much around me when I am talking with women. For some reason, we believe that we are to handle it ALL and not ask for what we want, or we have asked for what we want and have been denied it once or twice, so we stop asking.

This week, I know it is almost over, but take it through the weekend----ask for something you want! and then **_ALLOW_** it to happen. YOU are WORTH iT.

Tuesday, August 10, 2010

Text messages from Christi

We know text messaging has become the newest way to communicate when we have something little to say or we just want to send some love to those we know, and for my sister, Christi, she sends me little ideas and her thoughts about different scenarios she has had with her panties and her life.

A couple of weeks ago, she sent me one that said; "hey sis, what does it mean when you notice that many hours later, you put your panties on inside out and they have been like that all day?".

I had never thought of this one. So I sent back something along the lines of maybe it means you are not worried what others are thinking or that there may be some things in your life that you want to flip from the outside in.

She said, I think it is to keep those people out of my life that I just don't want to let in. I like it, was my comment back.

Yesterday, she sent another one asking me about going pantyless. She said to me, does it mean all is well in my life if I go pantyless?

This one deserved a phone call. My idea of going pantyless, is when nothing else will work. Labeling your panties just isn't cutting it and you feel like you are always irritated by one thing or another, this is when I would suggest going pantyless. Going back to when you were a new born and you knew nothing of beliefs yet, or how the world treated one person differently than another or what you knew to be beautiful or not. Thin, heavy, nice, mean, you name it, we did not know it at birth. We just were loved and held close without any conditions, most of us, that is.

Oh, she said, that is different than what I thought!

I realized something at that moment.....

The book I am writing is just the beginning for individuals to create their own panty world and use the metaphor to what suits their life the best. It is about individualism---

If what works for Christi is that **pantyless** in her life is all things are going great, this is awesome.

In my life, when I am not thinking about my panties at all, is when I know I have been relaxed and enjoying the moment.

If I am over the top with handling life, that is when I take it to the extreme and go pantyless!!!

Thank you sis. I appreciate your support and your text messages of panties to me.

Monday, August 16, 2010

Self Appreciation

Today has been an incredible day and momentous occasion on the journey of creating Who'd You Put Your Panties on for This Morning?

I am to the point where I no longer am "writing" and I am moving forward with the editing part of this adventure.

When Karen, my writing coach/publisher, congratulated me, I was speechless, excited, nervous and WOWED. I think I sounded something like this....aaaaa, ok, wow, seriously? and then I said I would like to hang up and call my husband. Before she would let me off the phone she gave me a final direction.....

Stretch my right arm out in front of me and then cross it over to the left shoulder. Reach around and pat yourself on the back-----You did it and this is a huge day for you.

Even though I laugh a lot and sometimes it may look like I am not the most humble person around when I talk about myself, and I have a pair of panties that state...."it's all about me", it has been hard for me to genuinely talk about myself and give to myself love and appreciation.

It even took me a minute to do so today!! It felt different this time, I really did appreciate and thank myself for the work and the time that I have taken to get so much of what I have wanted to share with others down on paper. Some of it was not easy and some of it, I had to look at choices that I had made that caused some pain to those around me...I am not a big believer of going back to what has happened in the past, but learning from it and moving forward.

All of us have momentous days. What are you doing to celebrate yours?

Believe it or not, I took a nap and did some more floating downstream--it is so much better than fighting up hill currents.

Tuesday, August 17, 2010

Encouragement Between Friends

Last night I had a conversation with one of my oldest, closest, forgiving and enduring best friend. We are always sharing inspirations with one another and the latest book we have read that has assisted us in one way or anther. Since 5th grade we have played together, cried together, encouraged each other and believed in each other.

As we talked, she stated she has been very sick with migraines and just basic malaise. She has not been able to do the things that she is used to doing. Even running, which is her favorite, has been challenging. It is hard to not feel up to par.....I bet most of us have been there.

Later, I had an idea and sent her a text. I asked her to close her eyes and to visualize what her health would look like in a pair of panties. I was going to surprise her and send her a new pair of **health** panties to assist her in getting through the next few days.

The next morning she sent me a picture of her in her perfect **health** panties and described them to me---

Soft, white cotton, boy cut with a pink trim. Fit like a glove, most comfortable and look great. Basic soft, sensible and perfect for me.

My text back to her was, "dang, I wanted to buy you a pair and send them to you as a surprise, and now I have seen a picture of you in your perfect *health* pair of panties, I need to find me a pair of *self love* panties".

Her next text back to me was, "describe to me what your *self love* panties look like."

I sent back, *self love* panties to me would be bright blue with a light yellow lace trim made out of soft cotton, spandex mix. Preferably a thong, so I would not have to worry about where it would end up by the end of the day."

Before I knew it she was sending me descriptions of some *happiness* panties and *self love* panties she had just bought at Target.

I just really enjoyed this interaction between her and I. Her encouraging me and me, encouraging her. Sharing in each others wellness. Thank you Shauna!

This last week I felt Joy after an exciting acquisition in my life. When I picture my JOY panties they are iridescent pink, yellow, and blue....alive with love and satisfaction! Oh and for a an almost 64 year old, a sassy thong! That is way over the top for me!

D.O., Utah

I think of that conversation often...I still have that text you sent me about you needing to find some self love panties, as you were referring to "not comparing yourself to me"! It was an ah-ha moment for me also, because we as women harshly compare ourselves to other women and find any reason to beat ourselves up for not measuring up. Putting on self-love panties is a MUCH more peaceful option! And in doing so, you gave me permission to do the same!

S.V., Colorado

Monday, August 30, 2010

Back to School

It has been a crazy couple of weeks making sure all children are clothed, back in school on time and in all the right classes.

I also have started my new classes for the fall of 2010-2011. I am so excited. One is the Adolescent Development and the other; Marriage and Family Relationships. I always enjoy these classes because I get clearer than ever on different ways to address situations when they come up.

As for my book, I have moved past the writing phase and we are editing!!! it is so awesome. After that, will be the lay out, and continuous movement forward.

I do notice almost every day I am able to ask myself the question, Who did I put my Panties on for this Morning? Even as I am to such important movement in my book, and the professional feedback from others is important, I still want to state what it is "I" want for the book. Sometimes, in our minds, at least in mine, I think we struggle because they are the professionals and know what they are talking about, but that does not mean we clam up and forget to follow through with what we originally asked for.

Lets remember to ask for what we want and ask again and ask again until it happens for us!...Because it will and it will be the way we want it!

Thursday, September 2, 2010

Layers oF PanTIEs

After more than three different conversations with friends about the same exact thing in one day, I figured this is definitely something to think about and better yet, write about. Thank you gals.

What I was hearing and what I know very well myself, is how we will create so many responsibilities in life that instead of just wearing one pair of panties we have on layers, and layers and layers of panties each pair representing all that we have created in our life until what we have created is our own secure diaper.

An example of this in my life would look something like this:

The pair closest to my skin would the pair that I actually put on just for me.

On top of that would be-my husband, then a pair for each child, so that adds on four more.

Then there is finances, which adds on three more pairs...medical transcriptionist, Medical Assistant and cleaning.

Another pair for being a student.

A pair for writing and creativity.

And yet maybe even a few more pairs for maintaining a positive attitude while at work, assisting those around me and let's say, maintaining the yard.

All righty then, if I am counting correctly-in one basic day, I have a layer of 15 pairs of panties on. Oh my, no wonder why I get a little lost at times, and the pair closest to me is way beneath all of the others.

This is a good opportunity to shed some of these and really take a look at what I want to be wearing.

As I thought more about the diaper we put on in our lives, I can understand why it is we created it. COMFORT and SAFETY.

However, in order to have other things happen in your life, you have to be willing and take the risk to open up room for what you really want.

I will always be a mom and a wife. I will also assist others around me in a positive way and influence their lives. I love learning....

Where I want to shed is all of the jobs, the things taking me away from the things mentioned above. In order to create this, I have to be willing to step out on a limb a little bit...RISK and TRUST in what I really want to do which is write.

There is a way to get to those base panties...I am willing to get there are you?

Sunday, September 12, 2010

The Trusting Pair

Trust is one of those words I think is sometimes much easier said than done, especially if you have had experiences in life that have shown you otherwise.

I would take a gander and say that I bet most of us have had something like a non-trusting experience we dabbled in some time or another in our lifetime. I realized one of my biggest ones today.

Honestly, I am not sure where it steams from, or even if I need to know the information, I am just grateful that I realized it.

The last couple of weeks, I have asked Karen, my publisher, to hold off on editing the book and sending it to her editor. I wanted to proof it myself and make any changes that I thought needed to be made even though she reminded me time and time again that she has people that will assist me in doing that and laying it out for me. For whatever reason, I insisted on doing it myself!

Today, I did find a couple of spots I indeed added much needed creativity but as far as putting things in a particular order, I surrendered.

This is when it hit me......It was time for me to rid myself of that old ugly pair of control top, do it all yourself and trust no one panties, for a pair of gold ochre, no worry, cotton, low rise briefs.

What a relief. It is not just this one area, the book, I can use this any time I am struggling with trusting another.

WHAT DO YOUR TRUST PANTIES LOOK LIKE?

Tuesday, September 14, 2010

Time OUT please!

One of my favorite people to listen to is Esther and Jerry Hicks. I have learned so much from their personal experiences and have created one of my own from what I have heard from them.

They talk about "upstream thoughts". Basically these are thoughts that a person has that are not necessarily going to do either party good by stating them, but more than likely cause a possible argument.

What I have come up with, is a "Time out Please" pair of panties that I hang on the doorknob of my room. That way everyone knows I just need a moment, two or maybe even 30 minutes to make sure I don't go spouting off "upstream thoughts."

Typically for me, I am not even really sure what happens to put me in these moods. All of the sudden I will walk through the door, see something on the countertop I think should have been cleaned up before I got home, and then it hits me....I feel it from the tip of my delicately painted toe nails, up through my abdomen and into the back of my throat to the point I want to vomit some horrible words toward the person standing within my path, no matter if they are the ones that left it there or not. All the sudden, my mind will see everything, every strand of dog hair collecting behind the plant pot in the corner of the room, to the toilet seat left in the up right position. I know that directly to my room is where I need to head because none of these things are worth the battle that I could create.

I look at this as a good time to take accountability for what may be going on for me and there is a more gentle way to approach it then the poison that might fly from my mouth at that moment.

To my room I head, hang the panties on the door knob and re-think about what my "upstream thoughts" are really about. It takes time, and it takes a new way of thinking.

Try it! When you are in one of those unknown moods, hang a pair of panties on the door and take some time to let go of those upstream thoughts.

Thursday, September 23, 2010

Gratitude

I am always out preaching to my friends, husband and sometimes those people I don't even know, well.....you know, ***Gratitude for what you have will always attract more.*** I was of course talking about the basic things one might encounter on a day to day basis: Money, love, help from a friend or family, a good day at work or that a child said please and thank you.

Oh, how I have seen the light today!!!

I bet you are wondering what I am talking about! Me too actually.   No that is not true. However, this is one topic I currently do not exceed in all that well and that is being grateful for ME, my accomplishments, my victories and my soon to be published, Book!

Even, as I write this, I take note of the reaction of my body; my chest is rising and then plummeting into my abdomen that I hold taunt. My fingers are leaving sweat prints on each individual key as I strike the specific letter that I need. I can even smell the sweet scent of the Vanilla Suave deodorant that I applied this morning as it works overtime to keep my arms from sticking to the side of my body......and my mind thinks heavily about darting out the bedroom door that is ajar 15 feet from where I sit....

WHEW-time to get Jordan from football practice!

Ok, now that I have had a chance to regroup and put on more deodorant, what I am saying is today I realized how little it is that I actually have gratitude for the things I have achieved in my life. It is like I have taken my celebration panties and hid them in the depths of my drawer.

I am aware as to why I do this, hide them that is, and that is the light I am talking about. I do it because I do not want to be boastful. But why not, is what I have to ask myself. Being a best selling author is what I have talked about for years and I am on my way!!!

Celebration, self gratitude and a whole lot of self praise are here! and I am ready to allow myself this.

I have my "SUPER ME" panties on and I am ready to head out into the world as the creator of the "Panty Revolution" and my book!

What about YOU? Where can YOU start being grateful for YOUR accomplishments? It can be anything--it can even be that you got out of bed this morning!

GRATITUDE FOR YOU will ATTRACT MORE OF YOU!!!!

CELEBRATE.

Wednesday, September 29, 2010

REALLY?! You don't do it the way I do?

I think this is one of those topics we all can relate to. I have really been just smacked in the face with it lately and been doing my best to allow the people in my life to do things and be the way they are--not the way I am or the way I would do things.

There is no doubt there will be plenty of "OOPS, there I go again". And I am really okay with that as long as I am conscious of it and step back a moment and let them be them. After all, that is what I talk about when I am talking about putting your panties on for you.

Even though I do not mean to, the reality of it is often times, I am asking someone else to put their panties on for me and do it my way.

This can be in the realm of so many things. For me it is about things like when the garbage should get emptied, when I would go to bed if I had to get up at 3:00 am, not going to work when I am sick, and excitement about fabulous opportunities in life.

Those just touch on some of my personal Could You Please Put your panties on for me Moments.

When I am fretting on the fact things are not happening the way I think they should, my stomach gets tight, twisted and vomit touches the back of my throat. My thoughts are angry and rather than acknowledging any greatness about that person, I am repeating over and over again, what they don't do and how they don't do it. My whole beings is uncomfortable, and trust me, they know that I am incredibly disappointed by the way I turn my back to them. Before I know it, I start hurling out a million why questions, followed by a statement such as, "I would take the garbage out before it was that full and you have to get up in 4 hours, what are you thinking?"

Yea, a NO!!! This only makes them not want to do things, and my pay off-- panties in such a tight wad, that it is strangling my happiness, keeping me on edge and stopping any type of succession of joy. Only here and there will trickles come through.

Mastering this new consciousness and zip of the lips can indeed take some practice, but it can be done. To really stop and think, why I am **NOT** letting that person be that person?

What am I telling myself because they don't do it my way?

and....

Is it worth the payoff that I am receiving from being so uptight?

I ask you, how do you feel when they ask you to be someone else or change something about yourself? And is the feeling, the one taking control of your whole being, worth it?

Monday, October 11, 2010

October

I just realized I have not posted anything in just over two weeks. Well, I must say that part of my reality is not being able to post all of the time even though I love doing it.

I have recently reviewed section 5 of the manuscript and adding sketches where I feel like they belong. I have to admit I am just barely starting to feel sooooo much excitement about getting closer and closer to publication that I feel like it is time for me to explode with delight. It is interesting how my thoughts and feelings about having dreams come true have just kind of kept me holding back but let me tell you---I am ready.

As Diana Ross so beautiful sings "It's My Turn" and "I'm Coming Out."

My life is delightful...and to think about what I am creating is like taking a bite into a slice of Kahlua cream cheesecake from Marie Calenders. YUMMMMMMY! and smooth.

I am not just talking about the book and the upcoming publication, but everything. As I read, write and study, I am learning so much about myself and how I interact with others. My, how life is fun when you can be intuitive to what is happening within you and willing to move forward off the back burner!

When you start to notice that YOUR shift is affecting those around you; husband, children, peers, co-workers and anyone and everyone---you shine from your soul out and the light from outside fills your soul.

These are the days that my panties fit to a T!

Wednesday, October 20, 2010

When the Past Knocks

Just yesterday, and it had been quite a while since this had happened, I had an ever so slight knock from my back door. The back door I am talking about is not made out of wood, nor does it have a handle on it with a lock, the back door I am referring to is that of past experiences.

It really did take me off guard, so let me explain it to you just a little bit!

The last few days I have been back to the routine of getting up early at around 3:50 am. I was now on my second early morning awakening with a late bed time the night before. Jeff, my husband, drives a truck and really is always easily accessible when I need to talk with him by cell phone. When I got up, like always, I gave his cell a ring; no answer. No big deal originally! It was after 2 hours, 2 texts and at least 5 phone calls, I finally got a hold of him. By then my belly was tied up in knots as I created in my mind the worse scenario I could imagine! and my mood started to act upon this.

When I did talk to him, I was not so nice, short and irritated, not to mention I was on my way into the hospital for a full day of work.

There are always a couple of the Women's Council there before I arrive, I was on the edge of tears because of the way I had treated Jeff, but I did not want to share that with anyone, I just wanted to get on with the day and apologize when I had figured out what was going on for me! Of course, the early morning gals noticed....I was not bubbly and what they experience me to be daily.

The final straw that broke my awareness was a loving text from Amanda; I set the phone down and headed into the restroom where I sat crying...

I realize my past experiences, were gently knocking, and creating self defeating behaviors. i.e. picking an unnecessary fight with Jeff.

This is when it really kicked in, "Amy"; I said inside of my head, "why are you writing a book if you are not going to follow your own life coaching?" I looked down at the maroon, lace cotton thong that was sitting just above my knees and labeled them what I needed for the day-----"SELF FORGIVENESS".

It is so easy to forget until something triggers you and rattles the handle on life's back door a bit, in the present. For some it might be a gentle knock, while for others it may be a hard core rap! Either way, it is a chance to make a different choice. The past is just that, the past!

I was grateful I had this experience, it reminded me sometimes something from then, might come up today, but being aware of what is going on is what represents such good opportunities to learn and move forward.

Self Forgiveness is vital to personal growth. Think about it, do you call something you learned from a "mistake" or an opportunity for growth...I say the 2nd!

Forgive and move forward!

Monday, November 1, 2010

The 11th Month

Happy November 1, 2010. WOW, how time really moves when you feel it with so many things.

October was great and now we move into a time of many birthdays in the family, my two boys, my sister's, my mom's and mine; not to mention several others. Then comes Thanksgiving and before we know it, Christmas will be here, as well as a New Year.

I love all times of the year, but this is one of my favorites. Our first snow fall here in Utah happened last week and it was incredibly beautiful. I am not sure how much the trees enjoyed it because they are still covered with leaves.

I am very focused on listening to the "Build a Thriving Practice" by Karen Curry, who is also my publisher. There is so much knowledge and information within these modules. I am also finishing up and allowing a place within my soul, exhilaration with my book, *Who'd You Put Your Panties on for This Morning* and the closer it gets to publication. We are still shooting for December!

I have had many experiences of labeling my panties and reminding myself who I do indeed put them on for. It is becoming such a natural cognitive awareness, that I do not always have to stop myself in order for it to work, my brain knows what to do and my physical body, as well as my heart just fall into line! It is awesome to be in this open space.

There is always more to come with the blog---and with the stories.

Panties on Girls, life is full of greatness!

Tuesday, November 2, 2010

The Final Section

This morning when I opened my email, I found there to be 17 new emails waiting to be open and read. I knew most of them would be comments from people about the new Facebook postings I put up last night, and since I feel I have been impatiently awaiting the last couple of sections to proof read of the book, I had no expectation what so ever they would be there!

Low and behold, amongst those 17 Facebook comments, was an email stating "Last Section!!!!!" I have to tell you, I just sat stone cold in my chair and looked at those words...regurgitating them, last section, last section, last section!!!

I totally opened everything else first. I slowly walked into the kitchen and retrieved my lap top and my flash drive from the bag I carry with me always, turned it on and opened the email.

As I have been reading this last, most beautifully pieced together section, visualizing where the newest sketches from Tara will fit into place, I notice that my finger tips are numb, there is a lump in my throat and I am not feeling much excitement at all----

Wait a minute Amy, what is going on for you right now? I stopped reading for a minute, opened up blogger and decided this is an exact moment in time to blog what is going on for me. I am lucky enough and have tools enough to take a real deep look at what is happening for me right now and what I can do to rectify the situation so I can celebrate. This indeed, is why I created the book in the first place, so I can take an old fear and spin it around into something beautiful, rewarding and joyful.

Now is my chance. Big deep cleansing breath in, old scary, I am not worth success breath out. Over and over again, until I am breathing pure joy into every point of my body and out the end of my toes, finger tips and top of my head.

I relaxed my hands next to my body in an open, receiving position, uncrossed my legs, closed my eyes and allowed myself to just be and to receive.

I visualized myself in a pair of low rider, bell bottom jeans, tank top, flip flops, toe nails newly polished as well as my hands freshly manicured, and there I am with a huge grin on my face signing my name on the inside cover of my finished manifestation.

I took my time, I relished in this moment, I could feel warmth all around my body and filling my hands as well as my soul. IT is indeed MY TIME.

I am not sure how long I held this position; I knew there was a moment in there that I cleared my mind of putting any time limits on this experience. The soft tears that filled my eyes rolled down and met the corners of my smile. Chills ran over my body as I opened my eyes to a whole new day!

I am there! I have created my dreams and believed in myself and trusted others around me!

It is truly a day of celebration, if it wasn't 6:35 in the morning, I would head for another pair of celebration panties to mark, yet, another fantastic moment in time. However, I am going to stick with my first set of celebration panties! Remember how in one of the other blogs I wrote about the bra not fitting? Today, I will use this for my advantage. Instead of allowing it to bother me, it will perfectly remind me--I am celebrating!

Can I just say, Start wearing your "BELIEVING" panties and see what you can create!

Thursday, November 4, 2010

ThanK YOU!

When I logged into ThePantyRevolution last night on Facebook, I found that my number of "Likes" has almost doubled over what it was just a couple of days ago.

I had chills run over my entire body---there are new faces there of women that I do not know as of yet, but am excited to get to know and from states all over, not just Utah.

It is indeed happening; my thoughts, experiences and intuitions are starting to touch others lives!!! It is really exhilarating.

More than anything, I want to just say THANK YOU to those of you that are new and to those of you that have been with me and inspiring, rooting me on and encouraging me from the get go.

I APPRECIATE YOU!

Monday, November 22, 2010

Checking IN

One would either laugh or scream if they saw me at this exact moment. I am sitting at my computer desk, comfy in a pair of gray sweats, my favorite red tank top that sports brown paint in the upper right hand corner, blonde hair dye on my gray roots and a cucumber mask covering my face, revitalizing my skin and currently covering my several kisses from the sun. I am indeed a vision of pure delight!

I have been incredibly busy trying to multitask the last couple of weeks, and P.S. an ever so loving counselor once told me that there is no such thing. I am learning over and over again she is right. Why? Think about it, if you are multitasking, that means one thing, maybe two or possibly three things in your life are typically not getting fully finished.

The good news is, we are the ones that can change our destinations and do less of the things we don't want and more of what we do want, for some of us, like myself, it may take lots of practice and reality moments before we start letting go of two, three or even four things in life to focus on what is most important.

Today, it is me, that is why I am sitting here indulging in the beauty and writing in the blog. This is what I would prefer to do; drink coffee, rub a cucumber mask on my face and blog, write and create.

As for now, I am working towards this. I am at the end of a school semester; I have been incredibly overwhelmed by this. Every semester I do this to myself---I put on the same pair of "do too much" panties and end up stewing in them. I am grateful that I can see that I am doing that and will be more mindful of next semester to be sure to let something else go before trying to add college into my list of multitasking.

Is there something you can let go of to get you out of the "I do too much" panties into some relax fit, cotton baby blue "ENJOY" panties?

Think about it, and go for it!!!

Thursday, December 2, 2010

ABUNDANCE in all of LiFE

I just wanted to do a small entry, as I am the end of a school semester and finishing up finals, papers and reading along with doing so many other things.

The excitement of creating continues to pave a path for me. It is not just the book but what can be done around the book to assist others. It is challenging in my mind at the moment only because making the choice to believe in such a big picture and a whole new life of doing what I want to do, has only been a distant dream and as it becomes closer, a whole new thought pattern and new panty labeling begins.

I often wonder if those that automatically have everything, had to think or feel much about it. I may not ever know that answer. I do know that even though there have been moments that I have thought to myself, "wouldn't it just be easier if I just didn't know", I would not trade going through every moment that I have in order to create this new moment.

Today is a day for ABUNDANCE panties. I am not only talking financial—I am talking everything. ABUNDANCE in my relationships with family, friends and co-workers. ABUNDANCE in my health and ABUNDANCE in life.

Saturday, December 4, 2010

PuZZlinG

Sometimes I just don't get it. I wish there was a way I could always maintain peace in my soul, and sometimes, I just don't.

As I sit here, I am not sure what is bothering me. I know that it presents in tears welling in my eyes and grazing my cheeks, as well as nausea. I keep wanting to label my panties to pull me out of it but today, right at this moment I am not even sure what I need.

In my mind I keep hearing Karen telling me to keep it real. That is part of life. Somehow, I keep telling myself life should go just swimmingly and I "should" be able to handle, know and control anything coming my way! And fix it when it happens.

Well, guess what, sometimes I do feel sad, and I do not even know why. or sometimes I am just angry and can't figure out what it is that got me that way and sometimes I am just mellow, without laughing all the time or socializing and that too is what it is and this is indeed okay. I get so caught up in "trying" to figure it all out.

The strangest thing just happened. After almost a year and a half I just received a call from Sally. She is the most amazing counselor I have ever had the pleasure of interacting with. She called to celebrate the book and in the quick 7 minute phone call got an ear full of what is currently happening for me. She did not try to fix it and said simple words to me; words I tend to forget easily...."it is okay to just be where I am. I do not need to figure it out right now! I can just be and maybe never figure it out".

I have had this chat with other gals I know. We have so much knowledge that it is not often enough that we just allow ourselves to be where we are. We attempt to make sense of where we are at, more so it ends up that we are self abusing by analyzing and not being ok with the fact we have chosen contrast in our life, as well as peace and joy. This is just a moment of contrast---nothing to fix, analyze or even worry about.

Today's panties---let it be what it is--and I trust!!!

Friday, December 17, 2010

The Last Few Weeks

This morning, I am sitting in my favorite room of the house, my front room. The only things that currently light it is the twinkle from the green, yellow, blue and red mini lights that hang on our Christmas tree and the mantel of the fireplace. I can see out the large window into the darkness of Utah at 5:45 am and the highlight of a large tree branch that holds a tiny amount of snow from the last snow fall on Monday. There are 12 plants in this room, all of them thriving. Gunner lays at my feet and protects me from any outside things that may head my way. I wish that he could protect me from my own thoughts sometimes.

The last couple of weeks have been rough for me. I have actually felt overwhelmed every morning by just waking up. Not a good way to start my day, I might add. No one would really ever know though, maybe Jeff because I find myself snapping at him for loving me. I do not like people to know that I do not have it all together or that I am struggling with finals, a couple of jobs, keeping up on things at home, proofreading and even the disappointment that I have had to change a couple of ideas that I originally had for my book, and waiting, waiting, waiting to hold my creation in my hand, and then still waiting. It becomes a horrifying, downward, out of control feeling of spiraling and not knowing where you are going to land.

More than anything, my thoughts become destructive because with all the tools and knowledge I have, I think that I should not ever go through moments like this, especially not for weeks at a time.

Here is where I have to stop because it is really affecting so many other things in my life, more than anything, how I feel about myself and if I am not loving me, then I am certainly not able to love anyone else around me!

Then when Karen mentions something like putting together a workshop in February, I start to doubt that I have anything to teach. Even though I know that I have chosen to have contrast in my life, I would rather be able to wiggle my nose and be back to the grounded, centered, dynamic woman that I have become.

Overwhelm looks something like this for me; I start to forget things, I miss whole chapters of work in my schooling, my test scores go down hill because I am not studying or focused enough to even read all the way through the question, I just want to get it over with. I throw things away that we need and I can't remember where the secret place is that I might have put it for safe keeping. Work feels like 100 hours rather than 9 hours. It takes me 5 days to string lights on the Christmas tree, and laundry piling up, brings me to tears and an unreeling bout of bitchiness. I start forgetting to breathe. My body will ache in weird places. Bed time is at 8:45p.m. I don't want to wake up to face a day and patience, is not a word in my vocabulary. I don't want to proof read or type any medical dictation and I start to, one at a time, let things go that need to be done and find myself not wanting to do anything but sip a glass of wine and stare at a blank wall. Not the greatest place to be, that is for sure.

This indeed started a couple of weeks ago for me. I remember sitting at my computer desk with tears filling my eyes, spilling over and then repeating themself. Out of the blue, I received a call from Sally, who is one of my all time favorite, most inspiring counselors. She first asked me to take a look at the stories I was telling myself and if those stories were true. Then she reminded me that it is okay to just be were I am at. This is the part of learning and life I forget about the most. To just allow myself to be where I am and feel what I feel.

I have realized I can only do one thing at a time in order to get something done the way that I want it to be done. This showed more in my lack of studying in my classes than anything. Frustrating to take two classes that I really wanted to take and not be able to put more than 3% effort in to them.

Here I am this morning, still in a little bit of a funk, having to walk away from writing this blog a couple of times and then coming back to it. However, I have taken my stack of papers, that consist of my writings of my book. As I flipped the pages, I found the one illustration that I have seen in my minds eyes for days and continued to ignore...

It is a gal, sitting on the toilet; her head is in the downward position cradled in her hand. The writing that goes along with the picture is about our beliefs and how at the oddest times, they will creep back into our life. I remember when I first had this visual come to my mind, my thoughts that went along with it were, "Oh no way, not again. Why am I going through this again?" Well that, my friend, is how I have been feeling for weeks.

I re-read what I wrote so I could follow my own instructions....I feel like I am ready now— FEEL what I am feeling

go back, start over

Remember I have choices in the now, no matter what the then was full of even if the then was two weeks ago or moments ago.

Visualize
Breathe
Throw away
and rename!!!

It is time; I took a pair of panties from my drawer. They are hipsters, black stripped, and ride just high enough on my butt cheeks to be comfortable and way too busy for me with the multiple colors that covered the rest of the material. Just looking at them, I knew this represented to me "**too much**", which is what life has felt like lately to me--I labeled them "way too Much" and took them out to the big black trash cans, opened up the lid and disposed of them. This way, when this whole overwhelming feeling that I have taken too much on, I can bring back to my consciences the look of this particular pair of panties, how uncomfortable they felt even just to look at and where I threw them away. That way, if this comes up again, I can remind myself---hey girl, you threw those away and they are way out at the dumps now-leave them there.

I then went to my drawer and found a burgundy, laced thong. I labeled them: "ONE THING AT A TIME" When I am at work today, I will focus on work. When I am at home, if I need to proof, I will proof and only proof. School is over so I do not have to be concerned about that. When I am with the family, I am with the family and not all over everywhere else and when I am with me, I will be with me, meditate, exercise and enjoy me!. I may have to label my panties this for a while until I really get into this groove but I believe that I will get there.

Oops, I am already doing it--I grabbed some food to eat while I type--I just set it aside to finish.

There will be days, times, moments that we find ourselves reliving what we thought we had conquered, and you know what, we will conquer it again!

Monday, December 20, 2010

My Christmas List --- FLEXiBLE

As I wonder around my house first thing in the morning; feeding dogs, loading the dishwasher, sipping on coffee or walking rather briskly on the treadmill, I am always thinking of something profound and savvy to post in the status section of the Panty Revolution Facebook Page. This is when making a personal Christmas list took on a new meaning. I thought about what I would want more than anything just for me (yes, world peace and joy forever are part of my list) but I am talking about things that are more tangible, that I have accountability over based on behavior and thoughts.

I decided that this week, since Christmas was at the end of the week on Saturday, that each day I would choose a word that either I think I may need a little assistance with in life or an intimate, loving and powerful word that I could glance at and remind myself of on a daily basis. By the end of the week, I will have a small start to something that I would like to continue throughout at least 30 days; giving me a positive word a day.

Today, the word I chose is "FLEXiBLE". I am not referring to bending over backward in a Yoga position either; although, that is probably a pretty good idea. Plus it would quite my mind...anyhow, back to topic.

When I picked the word, I was thinking that for me it is good because most of the time my actions and behavior are somewhat ridged. So, rather than the same routine of the morning where I am worried about time and getting everything scrunched in to a 2.0 hour time frame and running out the door with the feeling of anxiety in the pit of stomach, I just chilled and let things fall into place. FLEXIBILITY, FLEXIBILITY, FLEXIBILITY ran through my head as I just went on with each moment and it was easy and fun.

I walked down the stairs to find the kids snuggled up in blankets and sleeping soundly in their beds. I woke each of them and without pestering them to get up, get moving, brush teeth, get dressed and Hurray, I just walked away once I gave them the original nudge.

I got clear on why I do not allow myself to be FLEXIBLE too often, if feels to me like not caring and letting go of making sure all things run smoothly. In fact, as the morning went on and I was not walking back down the stairs to make sure kids were up, different things ping ponged back and forth in my head---what if they don't get up? What if we don't get out of here on time? **What if? What if? What If?** No wonder why tension, stress and tightness fill in my upper body creating golf ball size knots between my shoulder blades. Granted, kids do need to get out of bed for school, however, how I approach them getting up and allowing them accountability for their own adolescent behavior is a type of flexibility.

As the morning moved forward and things happened that I did not particularly care for, I reminded myself that I am willing to be flexible. Around 3:30, I was filling my water bottle and started to smirk...I could not remember my word for the day. I am not surprised to be honest with you, as slowly PMS panties were taking over. Not a pretty sight I might add.

Into the late afternoon and even evening, my Flexibility panties and PMS panties were at a slight war....PMS was winning by far. Amazing how they are so powerful. Even though I was careful not to snap at the family, I did.

I knew the only way to get back into my FLEXIBILITY panties was to get out of any panties at all and head for time alone in a bubble bath slightly scented with the smell of Sweat Pea from Bath and Body Works. This accompanied by a half glass of white wine and a little siesta and I was able to slip back into being FLEXible.

It took a minute but I was so grateful that the word I chose for the day was FLEXIBLE. In fact, it is a great word to start my list off with, as I realize that as I think back on the morning, I felt so much more relaxed and was enjoying the moment, just as it was. Not to mention, that as this week moves forward and I choose a new word for each day, I may run into some situations when I need to slip back into today's FLEXIBLE panties.

Looking forward to what word comes to me in the morning!

Tuesday, December 21, 2010

Patience

Well today was a success. I picked this word this morning after I had several trials with it—patience, that is.

It started out with just simple things like waking up at 3:30 am and wondering what word I would pick for the day and feeling a sense of urgency to pick it right then at that wee hour. By the way, I did not do it then, as I had several choices running through my sleepy head.

Next, I forgot I had turned the computer off the night before, and when I did start proofing, YIKES, lots of yellow and blanks of words the typist could not understand. It takes more patience than you can even imagine dealing with that, especially when the same typist has been typing this doctor for over six months.

After a few files, I went to add some blond to my gray roots, as I pulled on the teeny tiny plastic gloves that they always put in those boxes so the color doesn't hurt your skin; they ripped right down the middle. That is when I knew what I needed for the day--more patience than what I have had this morning and since, I know that the PMS panties were going to try to sneak their grumpy and irritated existence back onto my body, PATIENT panties would be what I would keep nestled to my skin.

I found the morning to be fairly easy...not much patience needed there until it got to about a half hour before our Christmas luncheon and the smell of several homemade creations gently swept up my nose and my tummy grumbled. Gratification came quickly on that one and my belly looked 4 months pregnant by the time I finished indulging.

The second most challenging moment of patience was when I was about one hour, 23 minutes and 5 seconds from leaving work for 5 days. WOW, WOW, WOW. I felt like it was 100 hours instead of a short hour and a half.

The last and biggest challenge in patience I had for the day was wondering and waiting if my book would be at our home for me to hold, visualize and proof....well, lets just say, it is a good thing that FLEXIBILITY and PATIENCE are the two words at the top of the list because I will be remembering them until it gets here.

AS my head lightly rested on my pillow, I thought about my "what I am happy and grateful for".......one of the things I was grateful for was that I was able to have patience throughout the day. PATIENT panties....well worth my Christmas list wish.

Wednesday, December 22, 2010

Day 3-Relax

Today was the perfect day for me to pick to relax, as before I even started my day, from my bed I had everything planned out down to the second as what I needed and wanted to get done so I could spend Christmas Eve and Christmas day away from the computer. I had a very small amount of last minute shopping to do, a house that I wanted cleaned, gifts to drop off to the gals at work, a hair cut, exercise and typing. I was prepared-If I got up at 3:50 am, I would be able to get this all done.

The snooze button was my best friend when the music started playing at exactly 3:50 am, and then again every 10 minutes after that until I finally got out of bed and touched the floor at 7:23. Of course thoughts of "oh crap" ran through my head, as well as, "I could have gotten so much done in those 3 hours that I chose to sleep".

This is when I came up with my third word for my Christmas list panties....RELAX.

It made good sense to me. I wanted to start off my five day weekend with not feeling all rushed and truthfully there was no one thing that was on my list that was not something that had a specific time limit on it.

My day really turn out very nice. I just set my mind to RELAX and moved forward from there. Taking time in the morning to just mill around the house, sit down and type and when my butt got sore from that, clean for a minute and when I grew tired of that, and then I exercised and so on and so forth.

It usually is not so easy for me, as I am much more high strung than that and feel good when everything is done that I want to accomplish. However, none of these things on my "TO DO" list were worth the price of not just RELAXING and enjoying the day exactly how it unfolded.

Wednesday, December 29, 2010

Christmas List WrapUP

I know I am behind and I am perfectly okay with that, but I did not want to leave you hanging on what I finished up with.

Diligence, which to me is the same as staying focused, was easier than I thought it would be. I knew that I had to stay focused on doing my work without distractions so I could turn the computer off by noon on Christmas Eve and leave it off all the way through Sunday...I did it and it felt sooo good.

For Christmas Eve, I picked Excellent Health. I woke up that morning early to type up some urology dictation and I could not focus on the computer or stay awake. IT was a different type of sleepy though, it was that type that just tells you that something is not feeling exactly right. I took the day slow; slept for awhile and then typed with a nap here and there. I knew that I had to refocus on my health, as we had a bowling date with 4 children and our friends and his kids. Along with that, we had a Christmas Eve birthday to attend and stockings to stuff. I did what I needed to take care of myself and then put on my EXCELLENT HEALTH panties and the rest of the evening I attended with my head up and body feeling Healthy.

For Christmas day, I chose FORGIVENESS. That was not so hard, as I did not have much or many to forgive that day. The day was beautiful. We spent time with our family and Sirius Holiday music. I made an incredible fudge, peppermint ice cream pie with peppermint whipped cream. Jeff put in a ham and made scalloped potatoes for more of our friends and family to enjoy in the evening. We watched "Despicable Me" and "Salt" two excellent picks.

My Christmas list was fulfilled!!!

FLEXIBLE-PATIENCE-RELAX-DILIGENT-EXCELLENT HEALTH-FORGIVENESS

All of these are very personal and powerful words for me. Words I want every day of the year.

Thursday, December 30, 2010

The FliP SiDE

All in all, I would call today a good day at work. I was able to keep myself busy and the time went by fast. Any mishaps that occurred were taken care of or my thought process was shifted from what may have bothered me, to something of a more positive nature. Sometimes that takes a minute longer than I would like, but the shift does happen.

However, today in the respects to my mind, it has consisted of many conflicts and by the time I got home, chatted with my best friend on the phone, picked up Jordan from the tracks station, dropped Golden off at his dads, picked some clothes up off the floor in the family room, cleaned up some doggy throw-up, and raised my voice a little bit at everyone in the house...

I found myself submerged in a tub full of steaming water, a glass of red wine cupped in my right hand and my thoughts bouncing back and forth and back and forth—

Looks something like this--what is my problem? wait a minute, I know what my problem is; everything happens for a reason; why can't she just communicate with me and tell me what is happening?; I know this is happening for a reason.; what can I learn from this?; oh, how I just want to go to sleep and float down stream; where is my proof of the book? There must be something wrong, or I did something wrong, but wait a minute, all things happen for a reason! Keep it real. Does it take this long? I am a new author; I don't know how this all works, but it seems to be taking so long! am I over reacting? This is ridiculous; I would be on top of this. Am I over reacting? Could it be that I missed it and it is a neighbor's house? will it be coming in the mail, why can't I just call and talk to the printing company? why doesn't she just call the printing company? I feel like an insane woman. Maybe another glass of wine would help or more hot water....etc, etc, etc.

OK, so you get the picture. Not a very relaxing bath, that is for sure. Something indeed did become very clear to me during this moment of mental ping-pong and steam....

I am a woman that for years, years and even more years, has pushed her panties aside, so to speak, when I have had a feeling that I would associate as being a "negative" feeling, and put on my "Happy Go Lucky", "Everything is Okay" or "NO Problem, I don't need to express myself, because it might hurt you or you might leave me" panties!!!

IMPORTANT MESSAGE TO SELF AND OTHER WOMEN WITH THE SAME PATTERN:

Part of the Panty Revolution, is allowing ourselves to feel what we are feeling!!!
This will indeed throw some people in our lives off as they are use to just stepping on us like the doormat that we have allowed ourselves to be for so long..

So, let me just state this here and now to get us started—

I am in some flaming, red hot anger and frustration panties at the moment due to the lack of communication about were and when my proof of my book will be here....

EXHALE...this is tough, my mind wants me to believe that it is not okay to express anger and frustration and my heart thinks that if I do, that people will walk away from me with all my dreams.

It is honestly an incredible amount of conflict. Now I know why I have chosen one of the three above mentioned panties before in life. It is less conflict.

The good news is as I allow myself to feel anger and frustration. I also get closer to hope and belief.

We all have FLip SiDes when it comes to how we may feel at different times. Honor those feelings, become aware of them and allow them to be by expressing what you want to or need to at that time.

INHALE.....EXHALE and tell it how it is!

Saturday, January 1, 2011

FLiP SidE 2

Just a little follow up on my story of the Flip Side.

It was different and conflicting for me to allow myself to be in my anger and frustration panties. It is honestly not one of my favorite places to be, but it is valuable to allow myself to feel what I feel, express it and WHEN READY and only WHEN READY, find a way back into a more comfy pair of hot pink, zebra stripped HOPE and BELIEVE panties.

My whole experience with writing, putting together, creating, believing and becoming a published author has brought many of my own past beliefs and fears to a place where I can look them eye to eye. At times they present to me immediately and I am able to clear them out quickly and at other times, I have been able to access tools that I have created myself or that I have learned. Sometimes, I even ask those around me for a little guidance.

Even though conflict is something we choose in our daily lives, it does not make it much easier when you are feeling it from the tip of your toenails out the top of those little stray hairs that stick up off your head.....

I called my mom to assist me with this one...I had my flaming anger and frustration panties on long enough, and she is a master at NLP and Emotional Freedom Techniques. I needed to shed one pair of uncomfy, but well needed panties, to a more pleasant, joyful and forgiving pair.

So if your time is up in the Flip Side panties---here is a way to get back to a place of peace within your body....It just works.

In one Column, write down the person, place or thing that is causing you so much conflict and write a list of all the positive aspects. In another column, write down all the positive aspects you can find about the whole experience. Allow yourself to feel the shift .the more positives you write down, the more shift will happen.

IF YOU ARE READY, and you have expressed how you feel; I invite you to do this little exercise to bring you back to YOU.

Wednesday, January 26, 2011

UndERgrouND

OH HOW EASY IT IS....to slip back into the realm of carrying and wearing the panties of so many others.....

The last week has felt like an eternity to me. The first proof arrived at my door at 7:00 p.m. via UPS one week ago today. Even though I looked like a lopsided chipmunk and a nagging ache consumed the right side of my face from the two hours I just spent in the dentist chair, I still managed excitement that the book in actual hard, hand holding copy was now resting in my palms. Then I opened it, Not what I expected at all...after all of this time, it was so not the way I had envisioned it...not even remotely close.

Anyhow, I have had an overload of emotions and realizations since I opened up the cover and started marking it up in red pen. In creating the book, the blog, a product funnel, Facebook, how to this, how to that, how to fit it all in and make it all work, TODAY IT HIT ME—I have somehow slipped into others panties, yet once again....

I am lucky I can giggle when I reread what I just wrote and I am grateful, for that is what the book is about: **Becoming aware and accountable.**

I am certainly not blaming anyone for this little slip--I am the one that allowed it and it reminds me even more the importance of being able to put a stop to it before you end up sick in bed for 5 days like I have been. All things happen for a reason, I do know this, and this little experience reminds me that it is time for me to step back, go underground a bit and focus on exactly one thing at a time. For me, that is creating the book the way I want it in my type of panties that I believe will work when I go to share it with you.

It may be a couple of weeks or longer, but I won't be keeping up on blogging, Facebooking, and product funneling...I will be UNDERGROUND getting back in my own panties!

REMEMBER--the GOOD NEWS is that YOU can always step back, take other's panties off your back and slip back into YOUR own!

If all else fails…
GO PANTYLESS

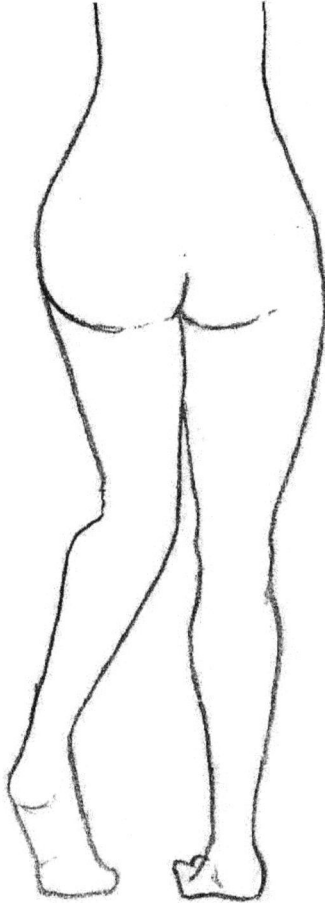

…step back into the world of a newborn and allow yourself to BE…

Who'd You Put Your Panties on For Today?

In my experiences, I have found the best way I deal with the real tough stuff in life, is to go pantyless.

There is no doubt, some days are only as hard as I make them and each day brings with it a new learning experience. What I do with those learning experiences is what keeps me within me, with the allowance of self forgiveness.

During these moments, I gently remind myself I have no panties on at all; just as if I am a baby within her first years of life. I know absolutely nothing of insecurities or worldwide societal beliefs.

I know nothing of love that is conditioned and no matter how I look, speak or act, I am always found to be adorable and sweet.

I have not been hurt and there have been no experiences of distrust, pain, criticism or negative beliefs holding me back.

As I approach my 42nd year of life, there is clarity in the fact I started where I was meant to be and honored to look back at a life full of so much growth, development, learning, maintaining glorious relationships and a new exhilaration as well as outlook on my life.

It is amazing to embrace the evolution of a dull piece of coal that now radiates as a polished, shinning diamond. What a fabulous life and I look forward to more to come.

I have created a glorious new and abundant life, building it to be exactly what I want my life to be. Filled with deep self love and value as well as smiles, laughter and unconditional love to go all around!

Going pantyless allows you to start where you are and create your blissful life the way that works for you!

Stories

Whether you wear white cotton briefs, silky hipsters, a colorful string bikini, spandex boyshorts or a lacy thong.....I bet at one time in your life, you may have put those on for someone else beside yourself.

Often times we do things for others at the expense, time, or happiness of ourselves. These are the stories that I am looking for.

At what time in your life did you do this? How did this experience look in the description of a pair of panties? How did you feel in that pair? What would you have rather been wearing? And how did it feel when you finally did for you what YOU wanted, creating your panties your way?

I want stories to share for upcoming books.

Sometimes I feel like I get stuck in a pair of underoos. I think most of us with children can understand this. Children, I think inherently, know how to manipulate a parent because we love them so much and we want them to love us. However, there are still boundaries you want set.

Have fun with this. Praise yourself for the new panties you did put on just for you and tell me about it!

Send stories to:
thepantyrevolution@yahoo.com

Who'd You Put Your Panties on For Today?

About the Author

Hello There! I have to say one of the things I have found to be the most difficult in my life is to talk or write about myself. For years, all my focus has been on what I can do for others, what their needs are and how my actions can make them happy. Today, however, I have a new story and here is a look at me.

I reside in Salt Lake City, Utah with my husband, our four children and two of the hairiest creatures that men call best friends, Daisy and Gunner!

My all time favorite things include:
Receiving gentle kisses from the sun, which present as hundreds of freckles covering my entire body, as I ride on the bow of our ski boat across the waters of Lake Powell.
Hiking the smaller trails of the Wasatch Mountains with the kids.
A silent chair lift ride through the snow dusted pines that drops me at the top of a perfectly groomed, wide ski hill.
The crisp air on a fall morning.
Four different, unique and inspiring voices coming from the back seat as the kids sing the latest hip song on the radio;

Laughing out load with my girl friends.
Matching bras and panties
Snuggling and holding hands with my sweet husband
The movie Charlie and the Chocolate Factory…it is a classic.

I have always been interested in psychology, sociology, social work and human nature, along with self discovery and self assertiveness. I worked as a psychiatric technician, and graduated with an Associates of Science degree in Medical Assisting. I currently continue my education taking only classes that I want to take and enjoy. Some of my favorites include Personality Theory, Human Growth and Development and Positive Psychology.

I am a true lover of life and the opportunities it presents to me so I can continue to grow and teach what I know and have learned, to others. I believe in asking for what you want and receiving it! And finally, I believe in the power of ME and my Panties.

www.ingramcontent.com/pod-product-compliance
Lightning Source LLC
Chambersburg PA
CBHW062040090426
42740CB00016B/2971